THE STONE AGE IN INDIA

THE STONE AGE IN INDIA

BEING THE

SIR S. SUBRAHMANYA AYYAR LECTURE

DELIVERED ON DECEMBER 10, 1925

P. T. SRINIVASA AYYANGAR
(FORMERLY PROFESSOR OF INDIAN HISTORY, ST. JOSEPH'S COLLEGE, TRICHINOPOLY)

GYAN

Published by

Gyan Publishing House
5, Ansari Road
Daryaganj, New Delhi-110002
Phone: 011-47034999, 9811692060
E-mail: books@gyanbooks.com

Distribution Network
gyanbooks.com
India, USA, Canada, UK, Australia, France

ISBN : 978-81-212-4548-7 (HB)
First Published, 1926

2nd Impression 2020

Printed at: Gyan Press, Delhi.

The book at your disposal is the edition of an old book originally published long back. The Text quality of this book may not be at par as compared to our other books but many readers approached us to reprint this important book so that it could satiate their hunger. We request all the readers of this book to help us to improve its quality by providing the necessary text of those pages which are not properly visible. Your valuable support in this case will be highly appreciated and acknowledged and our future readers will be benefitted immensely.

THE
STONE AGE IN INDIA

BEING THE

SIR S. SUBRAHMANYA AYYAR LECTURE

DELIVERED ON DECEMBER 10, 1925

BY

P. T. SRINIVASA AYYANGAR

(Formerly Professor of Indian History, St. Joseph's College, Trichinopoly)

MADRAS

PRINTED BY THE SUPERINTENDENT, GOVERNMENT PRESS

1926

CHAPTER I

THE OLD STONE AGE

THE ORIGIN OF MAN

After an elaborate discussion of the various finds of relics of early man and of the supposed precursors of man belonging to the Pleiocene Epoch, the latest subdivision of the Tertiary Age, which preceded the present Geological Period, in various parts of the world, the Rev. E. O. James, in his *Introduction to Anthropology* (1919), concludes: "it is quite within the bounds of probability that further research in the neighbourhood of the Siwalik (Sapādalaksha) hills in Northern India will reveal one more of the tertiary forerunners of the apes and man. *Palæopithecus* (i.e., ancient ape) may be cited as an example from the pleiocene of the Siwalik hills of a generalized type of extinct ape related to the Chimpanzee, the Gorilla, and the Gibbon, with upper premolars resembling those of man."[1] Since this was written scientific investigators have visited the Siwalik hills and have arrived at the conclusion that Northern India was probably the first home of man.

The persistent search for the "missing link," which may be called the biological approach to the solution of the place of man's origin, has been inspired by Darwin's theory of the descent of man from a pithecoid (ape-like) ancestor by incessant struggle for existence, the survival of the fittest as a result of the struggle, so aptly described by Tennyson as "Nature red in tooth and claw," and the consequent perpetuation of small accidental variations of the characteristics of the individuals, the accumulation of which enabled one species to evolve into another. Under the impulsion of this conception of the origin of man, the *Pithecanthropus erectus*—ape-man who stood erect on his feet—became the object of scientific search. Between 1891 and 1894 Dr. Eugene Dubois discovered on the east bank of the Solo, a stream which rises among the volcanic hills in the centre of Java, a skull-cap, a human thigh-bone (left) and two molar teeth which he claimed to belong to an animal midway between anthropoid apes and man. This skull-cap has been much discussed by biologists; six authorities have held the skull to be human; six have decided it to be simian, i.e., to

---

[1] pp. 61-62

belong to a man-like ape, while eight have concluded that it is intermediate, i.e., a missing link.

Meanwhile the Darwinian theory of the origin of species is fast losing credit. H. Reinheimer, after a re-examination of Darwin's arguments, concludes "that neither philosophy, nor physiology, nor palæontology, lend countenance to Darwin's theory of Natural Selection."[1] Reinheimer finds that evolutionary progress is not due to competition but to co-operation, not to struggle for existence but to symbiosis. What Miss May Kendall in the *Ballad of the Ichthyosaurus* sings :—

"Ere Man was developed, our brother,
We swam and we ducked and we dived,
And we dined, as a rule, on each other—
What matter, the toughest survived,"

can lead only to degeneration. "The cardinal necessity of life is not so much for the organism to fit itself merely expediently to any and every new condition, but rather to strive towards the achievement of the purpose of life by obedience to some sublime law of inter-dependence and of inter-determination . . . Many monsters of the past have played for anti-social self-aggrandisement to their own extinction, and the existing types that play a 'lone hand' are penalized in many more ways than has hitherto been thought of. Intense individualism, although abundantly evident, is what one might term a 'back number.' But co-operation is in the line of success; it, so to speak, expresses the soul of things, and we must learn to estimate the morality of nature by its main tendency, not by its occasional deviations."[2] In other words, as the rishis of old taught, love and self-sacrifice underlie creation and are the law of progress.

Other objections to Darwinism are not lacking. The facts with regard to heredity discovered by Father Mendel and his followers cannot be reconciled with the assumption of the constant appearance of spontaneous small variations by Darwin. Moreover anti-Darwinians are pointing out that the geologists whom Darwin easily made slaves of his theory, have based their interpretations of the evidence of rocks, not on their physical relations but on the evolutionary hypothesis. Ever since Lyell, after a long struggle, yielded to the blandishments of the Darwinian view of evolution, some 75 years ago, geologists have been arranging the sequence of rocks and fossils to suit Darwinian theories, and Darwinians

[1] *Psyche*, January 1924, p. 260. [2] *Psyche*, July 1922, pp. 20–21.

have been quoting the geologists' interpretation of rocks as the greatest proof of their hypothesis—a splendid example of arguing in a vicious circle.

Hence it is much safer for the student of history to turn from the biological approach to the problem of the first home of man, to the anthropological approach to it. This may be made both from the *a priori* and the *a posteriori* standpoints. On the one hand we may discuss which part of the surface of the earth was best fitted to support primitive man in fairly large numbers when he first arose in ancient times. He could surely not have inhabited the bleak mountain tops of the Himalayas where man even now cannot live; nor could he have inhabited the dense forests that clothe the lower levels of the Himalayan mountains or the equally thick jungle region called Daṇḍakāraṇyam, which in those days stretched from where the Indo-Gangetic plain ended to within a few miles of Cape Comorin. The inner recesses of the tropical jungle, even to-day, many millenniums after man learnt to conquer nature and utilize or transcend the conditions of his environment, continue to be too unhealthy for human habitation and too thickly infested with animal and vegetable monsters for feeble man to flourish there. Nor could early man have inhabited the great river valleys of ancient India. In early days the beds of rivers were much broader and higher than they are now, and the regions adjoining them, far too marshy. The great Indo-Gangetic plain, however fitted to maintain a teeming population now that the rivers have hollowed for themselves a deep bed, and man has drained the soil for thousands of years and learnt to raise several kinds of crops, must have been in the far off past too much without covert to afford primitive man shelter against his animal foes, both huge and small, and too much water-logged to be fit for men to live and grow there. Man, therefore, most probably rose and grew in the comparatively narrow strip of coast between the jungle and the Indian Ocean. Here the land is of moderate height above sea-level; the jungle was too thin to enable early man's animal foes to infest it in large numbers; he could find shelter in bushes and on tops of trees. The climate was as equable then as it is now; atmospheric conditions did not require that his skin, comparatively denuded of hair, needed any protection in the form of dress, which he had to provide himself with, when later he spread to less favourable climates. The soil, not far from river valleys, retained enough water to meet the wants of early man, who for want of pots could not live very far from sources of water-supply. Moreover, "*Homo primigenius* was probably at first mainly a vegetarian, . . . It can be pretty safely assumed, judging from the teeth of the earliest skulls, and from the lack of implements, that prior to the Chellean age (the lowest Palæolithic Age) primeval man was chiefly a vegetarian, except for such flesh as was furnished by small animals."[1] The fruits and nuts which formed the main portion of his diet were available in plenty in the fringe of the Daṇḍakāraṇyam. The fact that primitive representatives of the four existing types of anthropoid apes—the Gorilla and the Chimpanzee, the Gibbon and the Orang-outang—have been discovered in Southern India, proves that here man ought to have risen and flourished in ancient times. The environment that suited these apes must have suited also early man.

This conclusion, reached on *a priori* considerations, is amply borne out by the results of the search for relics of early man conducted so far. It is unfortunate that this search has not been systematically carried out by State or private agency. We have to depend only on the reports of casual finds by a few officers of the geological survey, or of very few other gentlemen whose enthusiasm for the discovery of prehistorical antiquities of the Indian man led them to devote a few odd moments of their leisure for the purpose. Partly for this reason, bones or other relics of the bodies of primitive men have not been found in India. This is mainly also due to the fact that he lived in regions exposed to the fury of monsoon winds and tropical rains, which must have driven to the ocean what parts of his carcase escaped the voracity of carnivorous beasts and birds. Moreover, early man in India had not, as his European contemporaries had, to seek refuge in caves from the cold of the Glacial Epoch, for South India was seldom invaded by glaciers. It is these cave-dwellings of the European palæolithians that have yielded skeletons of different races. The six Glacial Epochs of Europe, enumerated by Professor James Geikie, were represented in South India by corresponding Pluvial Epochs, very wet periods which must have washed down palæolithic skeletons.

We have, therefore, to depend, for evidence of man's early presence in South India, on his artefacts, i.e., on things made by him. "By assuming the erect attitude," says James[2] "man became differentiated from all other animals by being free to

---

[1] James, *op. cit.*, pp. 65-66.   [2] *op. cit.*, p. 67.

pick up and hold or throw stones, etc., an accomplishment of the greatest value in the daily quest for food. With a piece of flint he could pound up his roots, berries, etc., scrape with a similar weapon the skins of the animals he had killed, dig holes in the ground for store-houses, or increase the warmth of his hut, and in later times could hollow out trees to make canoes. In short, flint or perhaps, a bone implement, was used for everything for which a tool could be used. At first a stone haphazardly picked up no doubt served for many purposes." Man began to manufacture tools for himself from when he began his career on this globe; and artefacts are better evidence of human presence than bones and skulls and teeth, for it is often difficult to decide whether these belonged to man or other animal of similar anatomical characteristics. When primitive man—*Homo primigenius*—first stumbled against a stone or hit his head against the overhanging bough of a forest tree, and instead of wasting his impotent rage in pounding the offending stone to dust or tearing that bough to shreds, he turned the experience to profit and learnt to fling that stone as a missile at an enemy or broke that bough and used it as a club, he began his human career on the earth. Man has been defined as a tool-making animal, and this is a sound anthropological concept. The tools of early man are much more reliable as evidence of his presence in a locality than the ambiguous skulls and doubtful teeth and thigh bones which biologists have so far relied on to fix the age or place of human evolution; and those who have been engaged in collecting early human artefacts are forced to conclude that man first appeared in, and has since, without a break, occupied, the edge of the Deccan plateau. This can be made evident if we mark on a map of India all the find-spots of palæolithic tools discovered so far.

TOOLS OF THE EARLIEST AGE

The clubs used by earliest men have not escaped the ravages of time, for wood is a material whose life is very short in the climate of India; and, besides, the Indian Termites (white ants) have a special fondness for it. Yet we may be fairly certain that Indian clubs of several hundred thousand years ago were not very different in shape and size from the weapons which Indian gods wield to-day. There is no god worshipped in India nowadays, either inside dimly lighted temples or in airy places under shady trees, either by the meditative Brahmanas or the toddy-sodden low-caste men, but owns as one of his divine implements and has wielded, according to legend, for offence or for defence, a big-sized mace with a long handle and a heavy globular head ending in a sharp point. Hence we may infer that primitive man's chief weapon was a club with which he smashed the heads of his human or animal foes ; and when they were at too close quarters for flourishing his club before he could gather momentum for breaking his enemy's head, he pierced his brains through his eyes with the pointed end. The forests of India, then as now, furnished him with plenty of very hard timber which could be used for the purpose.

It is difficult to decide when early man learnt to employ the bow and the arrow. He was certainly intelligent enough to discover that he could split the bamboo, bend one split half into a bow, tie a piece of tough, dried creeper or of the sinews of an animal and shoot long, hard thorns from it. The descendants of these primitive men, now living in the interior of the Vindhyan forests, are certainly expert bowmen and could kill a tiger with one arrow. The conditions of primitive life were such that men had frequently to fight with wild animals face to face; and the very fact that the race was not exterminated proves that they had as much nerve and as much skill in shooting with the bow as the modern shikari. The Indians of those far off days probably also used spears made of hard woods. The head of a long, hard stick can be sharpened against rock or burned so as to end in a sharp point: and the heart-wood of the *Hardwickia binata* (ஆச்சா) or the *Xylia dolabriformis* (இருள்) or other stone-hard woods with which South India abounds, can easily be turned into a spear. But none of the wooden tools of old India can reasonably be expected to survive the action of air and water, conjoined with the insatiable hunger of the omnivorous *poochies* that have always abounded in the land, not the least of which is the so-called white ant, whose pertinacity in destructive operations is so wonderful. Man soon learnt to make tools also of stone. "At first a stone haphazardly picked up no doubt served for many purposes. Monkeys have been observed to use stones for cracking nuts, etc., and therefore there is no definitely human mental activity in the performance of such an act. But as soon as man appeared, it was not long before he discovered that a shaped implement was more practical than an unshaped one, and he began flaking his tools to the desired proportions. The earliest tools must have been made by flaking or hammering a piece of gravel with another stone to improve its shape and adapt it for use. Such roughly hewn pebbles, nodules and natural broken stones showing work . . . have been called 'eoliths,' or early stone tools. The controversy as to whether the so-called eoliths found in Europe were not the work of man is still unsettled. Eolithic forms are constantly being produced by cartwheels breaking up newly mended roads, the concussion of adjacent pebbles, the effects of weather and other natural processes . . . It is therefore clearly impossible to say that a given flint owes its form to natural or accidental causes, such as weathering, movements of deposits, ice, crushing in landslips, etc., or if it was chipped by man."[1] So far eolithic forms of tools have not been met with in India. Why this form of stone implement should not have been made by eolithic people, "if such people there was is a puzzle hard to explain, for various kinds of siliceous stone nearly approaching flint in its peculiar and special form of fissibility are to be found in different parts of the peninsula, to wit, the many forms of chert in the Cuddapah and Kurnool systems, the jaspers of the Dharwar system, the agates of the Deccan trap and, lastly, the true flints found in the valley of the Vellār river in the north-eastern part of the Trichinopoly District. Flint is also procurable in Sind."[2] Perhaps the very idea of an eolithic people and of the necessity for the existence of an early stage of rougher implements to form the precursors of the finished types of palæolithic tools is due to a too rigid adherence to the Darwinian hypothesis of evolution by the perpetuation of slow variations. Evolutionary progress was often catastrophic, *per saltum*; the first faint efforts, the halting attempts at improvements in several directions are not discoverable; the invention of language was probably due to a sudden outburst of human intelligence. Similarly man might have stumbled into the art of making stone tools of the palæolithic type, without a preliminary eolithic stage of development. Moreover, the discovery of eolithic tools, if they exist at all, needs a very careful search by trained investigators such as have not yet taken part in the survey of Indian prehistorical antiquities. But till the existence of an eolithic people is definitely proved to be a fact, we need not be concerned about the lack of eolithic finds in India.

[1] James, *op. cit.*, pp. 67-71.
[2] R. Bruce Foote, *Indian Prehistoric and Protohistoric Antiquities*, p. 14.

Lithic tools are the chief evidence of man's residence in any locality and it is by noting the sites where they have been discovered that we can determine in what parts of India man first flourished. These first tools were made by chipping; pebbles were carefully selected from shingle-beds and, by a skilful blow or two with another stone, the required sharp edges were produced. Early man displayed a wonderful skill in shaping these tools; but he did not polish their surfaces. For a very very long time he was content to use rough-surfaced tools. Then he learnt to grind the surfaces of his tools till they became very smooth to the touch. The long lithic stage of human culture, whose length was many many times greater than that of the historic period, is hence divided into two parts, the first called the Palæolithic Age or that of the old, rough stone tools, measured in hundreds of thousand years, and the second called the Neolithic Age or that of the new, smooth stone tools, measured in thousands of years. Man's progress was at first slow, painfully slow, so that the first age of human history was as long as the Yugas of the Indian astronomer.

PALÆOLITHS

Palæoliths have been found chiefly in South India. The Kurnool district has yielded abundant palæolithic remains. Considerable areas of the coastal regions of the Guntūr and Nellore districts contain relics of man's handiwork. So, too, the hills, maidans, and scrub jungles of the Cuddapah district. The Chingleput and North Arcot districts have yielded innumerable palæolithic tools. In the Dharwar and Bijapur districts—the Southern Mahratta country—all sorts of fine implements of the old Stone Age have been picked up. A single specimen from the Narmadā valley (Central Provinces) furnishes decisive evidence of man's contemporaneity with extinct vertebrate fauna. In the Gōdāvari valley (Warangal division of the Hyderabad State) has been found an old factory of palæolithic tools. A few implements have been found scattered in Central India and Rajputana and almost none in Bengal, Bihar, and Orissa. This proves that from the earliest times man flourished in the edge of the Deccan plateau.

The Palæolithic Age in Europe has been divided into the Lower Palæolithic and Upper Palæolithic, and these into seven sub-periods:—(1) Chellean, Acheulean, Mousterian, (2) Aurignacian, Solutrean, Magdalenian and Azilian—called after the names of the places where the characteristic tools of each period have been discovered. When the higher palæolithic period began there was a marked improvement in the method of flint-working and various new kinds of tools, showing an increase in the number of handicrafts, were manufactured; new materials were used for implement making—such as bone and ivory. Sculpture on stone and engraving on bones were practised and the artistic sense of palæolithic man reached its highest point. Indian palæolithic artefacts—cleaving, smiting and digging implements exactly resembling the early Stone Age implements found in Northern and Southern Africa, Central America and in Europe have been picked up and stocked in the museums of Madras and Calcutta. Mr. J. Coggin Brown divides them "into three types, namely, *bouchers*, which correspond to the English 'Celt' . . . palæoliths, in which I include the axe and the cleaver-like forms . . . and discoid forms."[1] Mr. Bruce Foote, however, recognizes ten distinct forms of tools. They are (1) axes, of which four forms have been found—(*a*) pointed oval, (*b*) oval, (*c*) square-edged, called the Madras type, (*d*) oblique-edged, called the guillotine type; (2) spears—(*a*) narrow type, (*b*) broad-based type; (3) digging tools, pointed with thick pebble butts; (4) circular implements, hurling-stones with sharp edges all round, the prototype of Vishnu's *Chakram*; (5) choppers, pointed oval with sharp edge on one side only; (6) knives, long narrow flakes with parallel sharp edges; (7) scrapers; (8) cores; (9) hammer-stones; (10) strike-a-lights. "The palæolithic forms are at least ten in number, clearly designed for different purposes. The leading shapes are pointed ovals . . . These show considerable differences in the proportion of their width to length and have all sharp edges all round which would prevent their being used in the unprotected hand. They were in all probability fitted into cloven handles and securely lashed with gut or stripes of wet hide or strong vegetable fibre; but no type of hafting was preserved in the deposits in which the implements came to be buried."[2] The sharp-edged tools of the old Stone Age reveal that palæolithic men possessed much skill of hand; the cutting edge of these tools was made by the meeting of flake surfaces, each produced by one blow; repeated small chippings could not result in so sharp an edge. A few of these tools have a blunt edge, for they were meant to be grasped by the unguarded hand when used.

---

[1] *Catalogue of Prehistoric Antiquities in the Indian Museum*, pp. 1-2.

[2] Foote, *op. cit.*, pp. 9-10.

By far the greater number of palæoliths that have been discovered so far in Southern India were made of quartzite, the most suitable material and the most largely developed in the North Arcot, Chingleput, and Nellore districts. Quartzites are "metamorphosed sand-stones, the metamorphosis consisting of the introduction and deposition of secondary silica, in crystalline continuity with the rolled quartz-grains of the original sand-stone."[1] Several great shingle-beds afford widespread supplies of shingle in Southern India, especially in the East Coast. Quartzite was the most suitable material for the purpose of making tools; and "north of the valley of the Pālār river, it was far and away the most plentiful material; the great shingle-beds of different ages of the Jurassic rocks (the Rajamahal series), the Sripermatur and Sattiyavedu series, afford inexhaustible and widespread supplies of splendid shingle, which the palæolithic folk seem to have preferred greatly to masses of quartzite broken off from the vast beds of that rock which give rise to the enormous scarps which figure so strikingly in the Cuddapah and Kurnool systems as seen in the Nagari mountains and the Vellikonda and Nallamalai ranges of the Eastern Ghats."[2] But west of longitude 77°30 W, true quartzite "is not found in any quantity and the old stone chippers had to content themselves, unless prepared to undertake a long and perilous journey, with the best substitute they could find, which in Bellary district was the more siliceous varieties of the hæmatite quartzite which forms such huge beds in the Dharwar system to which belong the hill ranges in the centre and western part of the district. It lent itself by no means so well to being worked into implements as the true quartzite, but still the old workers managed to turn out useful axes and other tools."[3] A few palæolithic tools of quartz have been found in the Gōdāvari valley and the Baroda State; but quartz lends itself very badly to being chipped in any shape. In the Rewah State, the palæolithic people made their tools of porcellanite, "a kind of hornstone or baked shale which occurs in the lower Vindhyan rocks of this region."[4]

HUNTING

Man began his career on the globe as an eater of fruits and nuts. This is proved by the facts that his food tube is long, his tongue is smooth and his teeth are flat, whereas the flesh-eating

---

[1] Wadia, *Geology of India*, p. 72.

[2] Foote, *op. cit.*, p. 9.

Foote, *op. cit.*, p. 77.

[4] *ib.*, p. 101.

animals have a short tube, pointed teeth and a rough tongue. Moreover, since the taste-buds that form the extremities of our taste-nerves have been evolved with reference to our natural environment, fruits and nuts, which contain all the food-stuffs necessary for man (and the latter, the fat required, in the easily assimilable form of natural emulsions), are of sweet taste and agreeable flavour. Besides this, fruits contain acids that kill disease-creating germs that may accidentally find lodgment inside our bodies. Fruits and nuts still continue to be sweet and agreeable to the tongue, though man has, during many millenniums, been vitiating his nerves of taste by perversely training them to appreciate things which possess what one may call the unnatural tastes—bitter and burning, astringent and alkaline. Hence fruits and nuts are the best diet even for the modern civilized man. But early man found that seasonal variations affected the productivity of the trees and plants he depended upon for the supply of his food. The advance of glaciers on several countries of the then habitable parts of the earth also compelled him to search for other kinds of food. He found the flesh of animals to be tasty and thus acquired flesh-eating propensities. So he "added animal food to his original diet; but even so his earliest attempts at hunting would most likely be confined to frogs and the small rodents, till, as his implements, weapons, and skill became more developed," he grew in courage and entered the heart of the forest and became a hunter of big animals both for food and self-defence. This is proved by the fact that many choppers with sharp edges are found on many palæolithic sites; these were evidently used for cutting the meat of animals which palæolithic man killed for food. But yet, his principal food continued to be fruits and nuts and tubers; for human teeth are not as strong as, and human tongues are not as rough as, those of the meat-eating animals; with his digging tools he dug out of the ground the various succulent roots that are native to Southern India, and ate them with relish. For the South Indian did, as modern Indians do, subsist mainly on vegetable food and ate meat, only as curry, i.e., as an auxiliary to his vegetarian food, unlike the ancient and the modern European, whose principal food is meat and who regards vegetables only as an auxiliary, to provide a variety to the nerves of taste jaded with monotonous animal food.

But the axes, the spears, and the hurling-stones used by palæolithic man were not merely used for hunting animals for food. He had constantly to fight with the bigger animals, which would, but for his skill in hunting, have soon exterminated him. palæolithic man had certainly a hard time of it with his zoölogical environment. He had to contend against tigers (especially those that became the much-dreaded man-eaters and acquired the taste for human flesh which seems to have a special fascination for tigers), lions which probably were rarer than tigers, panthers and cheetahs which were numerous, hyenas and bears. The elephant, the rhinoceros, the wild boar, the bison, the wild buffalo, the crocodile, the python, the viper and the cobra must have also caused much mortality among early men. Sharks and other varieties of sea-animals must have frequently taken toll of human life. The smaller stinging animals—scorpions, spiders, wasps and ants—whose stings though they are not immediately destructive of life, certainly cause very much annoyance, abounded in the land then, as they do now. Hence palæolithic man's zoölogical environment was not very pleasant; but yet the innumerable dangers by which he was surrounded, stimulated his courage and made him an efficient hunter, expert in the use of the bow and the arrow, the club, the spear and the quoit. The life of the hunter certainly develops great keenness of the sense-organs, and the junglewalla of to-day and the shikari, who is so indispensable to modern Nimrods, have inherited from their stone-age ancestors their unerring sureness of aim and extraordinary keenness of senses and consequent general intelligence.

Descendants of palæolithic men, who follow man's first occupation of hunting are still found in various parts of India, more especially in the forests where they can exercise their profession. There is literary evidence to prove that former kings of India employed shikaris (வேடர்) when they hunted the nobler animals for amusement, as also for guarding villages in forest tracts from wild beasts; and even to-day foreigners who come to India for killing wild game rely on these jungle men who are expert with the bow and arrow. But their arrows have, since iron was discovered in South India, been tipped with steel arrow-heads, and they have learnt to use other iron tools. But otherwise they have not got over their palæolithic habits.

FIRE

"No traces of the use of fire have, so far as I know, been met with in deposits containing the oldest chipped stones, but their makers must have known it."[1] The reasons why palæolithic hearths have not been discovered so far are, first, that the old stone-age people chiefly lived in the open; secondly, the cave-dwellings where palæolithic man might have taken shelter, like those in Europe which have yielded evidence of fires which he lighted in the far off past, have not yet been explored. "The shapeliness and good workmanship, however, of many of their weapons and tools" show that they were a distinctly intelligent people, and very early in their career must have devised means of obtaining fire. Bamboo which easily ignites by attrition is plentiful in Southern India. Even now a strong breeze produces conflagrations in bamboo groves very frequently; and surely early man was intelligent enough to experiment in the generation of heat, and to invent the manufacture of fire by rubbing together two pieces of wood. Man soon discovered that he could obtain fire more easily by drilling a small hollow with a stone tool on a block of wood and churning a stick in the hollow. This, the earliest method of producing fire, has become the holiest, for the earlier a custom the holier it is, and later customs are considered worldly in contrast with earlier ones. So even to-day fire for the Vedic fire rite, *Yajña*, is produced only by churning it with a fire drill, *araṇi*, on a piece of wood with a hollow on its surface. It is only with such a fire produced in such a fashion that the cremation of the corpses of Brahmana men and women who have performed the Vedic rites of sacrifice, can be conducted even to-day. A later fashion of producing fire, devised when palæolithic man became more used to employing stone tools, was by striking flint and catching the sparks in inflammable material like the palmyra fibre. This is certainly a later fashion, because it has not acquired the sanctity which is associated with the former method. Both fashions of making fire can be observed to-day throughout India, where modern matches are not available. "Having discovered a method by which fire could be obtained, it would not be long before our primeval ancestors found abundant uses for this all-essential phenomenon. It would soon be ascertained that fire was a means of safety from the attacks of hostile animals, and that cooked food is more palatable than raw flesh. Little wonder then that, in process of time, it came to be regarded with superstitious awe as a gift from heaven."[2]

---

[1] Foote, *op. cit.*, p. 11. [2] James, *op. cit.*, p. 99.

The mystery of the birth of fire from the fire-stick filled the minds of the Indian people with inexpressible wonder which lasted for very many millenniums. In North India arose the Arya fire-cult, when, it is impossible to find out, and Agni came to be believed as the mouth of the gods — he, into whose mouth were poured the libations intended for the numerous gods worshipped by the Aryas. However often he was produced for the sake of the fire-ritual, the mystery of his birth never ceased to produce a sense of wonder. The famous Rishi Visvamitra, not at all an early Rishi, sang[1] :—

astīdam adhimanthanam asti prajananam kritam
etām vispatnim ābhara agnim manthāma pūrvathā
araṇyor nihito jātavedāh garbhaḥ iva sudhito garbhiṇishu
dive dive idhyo jāgrivadbhir havishmadbhir manushyebhir
uttānāyām ava bhara chikitvān sadyaḥ pravītā agniḥ vrishanam jajāna.

"(Here) is the upper fire-stick, (here) is the tuft of Kusa grass ready. Bring the matron (i.e., the lower araṇi, wood for friction) Let us churn out Agni as before. In the two fire-sticks lies Agni as the embryo in pregnant women. Day by day is Agni to be lauded by the men who are wakeful and bring him oblations. Skilled (in the work), carefully lay (the upper araṇi) on that which lies extended. Being impregnated, she speedily brings forth the vigorous (Agni)."

The familiarity with this process of making fire did not abate the sense of mystery in the production and immediate growth to large dimensions of fire and of his consuming the oblations intended for the gods. Rishi Upastuta sings :—[1]

chitraḥ it śiśos taruṇasya vakshatho na yo mātarāv apyeti dhātave
anūdhāḥ yadi jijanad adha cha nu vavaksha sadya mahi dūtyam charan.

"Wonderful verily is the tender baby's growth, who never draws nigh to drink his mother's milk. As soon as she who has no udder bore him, he, going on a great errand, suddenly grew strong."

In time the rishis saw the activity of Agni in heaven as well as on the earth. They worked out the analogy between the drilling of fire (*agnimanthanam*) and the act of *prajananam* and reached the

---

[1] *R.V.* X, 115-1.

idea of creative fire in the activities of the gods in producing the cosmos out of *asat*, the chaos which existed before creation. A rishi sang,[1]

asachcha sachcha parame vyoman dakshasya janmann aditer upasthe
agnir naḥ prathamajāh ṛitasya pūrve āyuni vṛishabhas cha dhenuḥ

"Not existing (actually), but existing (potentially) in the highest heaven, in the creative power of Daksha and in the womb of Aditi, Agni became in a former age the first-born of our rite and is both a vigorous bull and a cow." The history of the growth of cosmogonic speculation from the primitive fire-rite on Indian soil is a most interesting subject to work out, but this is not the place for this study.

A RACE OF NOMADS

No traces of palæolithic habitations have been found anywhere in India. Most probably the man of the Lower Palæolithic epoch did not live in houses. In Old India houses were first built not so much for shelter as for storing provisions, and early man lived on fruits and nuts picked from the living tree and roots dug from the ground, and had little need to store his food. What little food he had to keep for some time could very well have been buried in holes dug in the earth. No traces of pottery have been found associated with the implements of palæolithic man ; there was no necessity for pottery till man had learnt to plough the ground and raise and store crops, or to bury his dead. It is these that create attachments, utilitarian or sentimental, to particular localities. Primitive man was, hence, an absolute nomad, a great wanderer on the face of the earth. It has already been pointed out that the stone tools of the Palæolithic Age, all the world over, show a great family resemblance, and modern anthropological opinion is inclined to attribute this, not to accidental coincidence, but to an intimate intercourse between the peoples that inhabited the different continents of the world. Nowadays the idea of extensive movements of early man onthe earth is accepted by most anthropologists[2] Towards the close of the Palæolithic Age, men changed from a nomadic life to a more settled one. Even from earlier times the herd-instinct which is very strong in human beings, and the necessity for protection against animal foes, must have impelled palæolithians to live in small communities,

[1] *R.V.* X, 5, 7.

[2] W. H. R. Rivers, *Psyche*, October 1922, p. 122.

near the sites where they could find the stones needed for their tools. A study of the map of palæolithic sites "shows that the several peoples concerned were widely distributed over the country, excepting in the mountain and great forest regions of the west of the peninsula, in which so far as my experience goes, no traces have been found of the palæolithic race, or races. The localization of all the races has also been influenced in some measure by the distribution of the rocks yielding materials suitable for their respective implements. Thus, there are far more numerous traces of the palæolithic race around the great quartzite-yielding groups forming the Cuddapah series of the Indian geologists and the great quartzite shingle conglomerates of the Upper Gondwana system in the Chingleput (Madras), North Arcot and Nellore districts, than in other regions. In diminishing quantities traces of palæolithic man are found to the northward of the Kistna valley, where quartzite becomes a much less common rock. So also to the southward of the Pālār valley where quartzite becomes a rare material; to the westward on the Deccan Plateau, where the stone chippers finding no quartzites in the Bellary district had recourse to the banded jasper hæmatite rocks of the Dharwar system; and further north in the valley of the Kistna where recourse was had in one instance to hard siliceous limestone."[1]

Traces of Magdalenian settlements, belonging to the close of the Palæolithic Age have been discovered in the great Billa Surgam cave in the Kurnool district. Besides bones of extinct and existing animals, a number of pre-historic objects including pendants made of teeth, and a few carved bones were found there. Other caves in the great limestone areas of the Kurnool, Cuddapah and Dharwar systems still await the search of the investigator.

No doubt the men who lived in the late palæolithic settlements had developed a primeval social organization somewhat like the system obtaining among modern races of primitive people. This must have included a division into groups and sub-groups marked by endogamy, totemistic and magic practices; but little light can be gained with regard to these questions from the relics of palæolithians which can be discovered. The nomadic races and the jungle men of modern India no doubt retain some of the old world customs, and a systematic study of their beliefs and practices may throw some light on the problem.

---

[1] Foote, *op. cit.*, p. 36.

DISPOSAL OF THE DEAD

As primitive man was a wanderer, he probably abandoned the dead, wherever they dropped down, a prey to carnivorous birds and beasts. No traces of pottery have been found associated with the implements of palæolithic man; and when pottery first appeared in the Neolithic Age, it is chiefly of the form of burial urns and trays for the food-grains buried along with the dead. Disposal of the dead by abandoning them to the natural agencies of destruction continued in India to comparatively late times. The Vedas[1] mention among the Fathers invoked in the *Pindapitṛi-yajña* the *Paroptas* and the *Uddhitas*. The *Paroptas* refers to people abandoned in distant places, and the *Uddhitas*, to those exposed on elevated localities. Exposure of the dead persists to-day in a modified form among the Tibetans and the Parsis, and, in stray cases, it is met with in Indian History till the seventh century, A.D. Yuan Chwang, the great Chinese traveller, mentions three recognized customs in Madhyadēśa, with regard to the disposal of the dead, of which the third is "burial in the wilds, the body being cast away in the wood to feed wild animals."[2]

DRESS

Indian climatic conditions do not require that man should be over-burdened with impedimenta in the form of dress. Primitive man was stark naked, and even to-day reversion to complete nudity is an especial mark of super-holiness among several classes of Indian ascetics, and in many parts of India, even among the laity, men and women shed the pollutions of touch by shedding their clothes, as is evidenced by the custom of *Chikaṭi Maḍi*, lit. the sacramental cleanliness of darkness, i.e., the holiness of nudity, among Telugu people and others. When primitive man became a hunter, he began to cover his person with the hides of animals. The stone scrapers found among palæolithic tools were used for scraping clean the flesh of animals which the palæolithian killed for defence or for food; the hide was then dried and worn on the back. He also wore a garland of leaves round his waist as certain jungle-folk of to-day do. He also employed the thin inner bark of trees called in Indian languages "tree-flay" (ಮರತೊಗಟೆ) for the same purpose. Hence the skin of the tiger and the deer and tree-flay have continued throughout the ages to be the holiest form

---

1 *Atharva Veda Samhita*, xviii, 2-34. 2 Watters, *On Yuan Chwang*, i. 174.

of dress, next to nudity, for Indians. Siva wears a tiger skin, when he is not naked; rishis and other ascetics, such as Śrī Rāma and Sītā during their exile, wore bark dress, and in the Vedas the "upper cloth," *Yajñopavitam*, is defined as deer hide worn on the left shoulder.[1] Even to-day the Brahmana youth, who is technically a student up to the date of his wedding with a little girl, wears a bit of deer hide tied once a year to the thread that is the modern much-minified *Yajñopavitam*. And people who follow meditation practices sit on seats of unpollutable tiger skin or deer skin, when engaged in yoga.

This hide was worn on the left shoulder leaving the right arm free to fight against enemies in defence or offence. This is the origin, probably, of the *Upavitam*, the manner of dressing prevalent among the Devas, according to the *Āraṇyaka* referred to above, the human way being *Nivitam*, leaving both arms free and placing the skin round the right shoulder, the *Prāchināvitam* being the way of the Asuras, who were the enemies of the Devas.

THE SPEECH OF PALÆOLITHIC INDIANS

Speaking, like tool making, was one of man's early accomplishments. Philologists believe that the languages of early men were holophrastic, i.e., the whole sentence, unbroken into words formed the unit of speech. Such languages even now prevail among certain primitive tribes of South America. No representative of this form of speech is found in modern India.

But there exist in the more inaccessible interior parts of India, a group of allied languages, e.g., Sonthali, Savara, etc., to which Max Müller has given the name of Muṇḍāri. Nishāda is a much better name, for these people are the modern representatives of the ancient hunters and, in early Sanskrit literature, were called Nishādas. These Nishādas are even to-day in a very primitive stage of culture; they inhabit now, as in the Vedic Age, the inhospitable regions around the Vindhyan hills, to which they were driven by the pressure of the pastoral and agricultural neolithians who flourished and multiplied fast in the fertile river-valleys and the productive lands adjoining them. We may hence conclude that the speakers of Nishāda dialects to-day round about the Vindhyan region are the representatives of the palæolithic folk, and that these dialects have been evolved from the possibly holophrastic dialects of primitive Indians. The neolithic people

[1] *Taittiriya Āraṇayka*, ii, 1.

throughout India spoke dialects of the family of languages to which the name "Dravidian" has been given by Dr. Caldwell. It has been debated whether the Nishādha dialects are related to the Dravidian dialects, but the Nishāda dialects have not yet been studied by trained philological experts; the few notices we have of them by amateur philologers do not afford us satisfactory information about their essential structure, which cannot be well made out by mere word-lists, tables of pronouns and brief notices of accidence. Hence reliable conclusions cannot be reached regarding the affinities of these dialects. Only one thing is certain; the passage of the palæolithic into the neolithic stage in India was not marked by any catastrophic change; so far as we can judge, the change from the one to the other seems to have been one of peaceful evolution. Hence it is not impossible that the two sets of languages are intimately connected with each other. But the utter ignorance of philologists about how languages arose in early times and how families, other than the Indo-Germanic, changed in the far off past, forbids any speculation on the question.

ART

Drawings and paintings of men and animals, notable carvings in horn and engravings on stone made by palæolithic artists have been discovered in French and Swiss caves inhabited by palæolithic man. No such art products have yet been found in India except the pendants made of teeth found in the Billa Surgam cave of the Kurnool district. On this, remarks Foote[1] "It would be unsafe to conclude that none had been produced by the old people who were possessed of burins, or engraving tools, similar to those used by the palæolithic artists who drew the wonderful pictures of man and his contemporary animals referred to above. Similar drawings may have been made by the Indians, and have been destroyed by those ubiquitous destroyers of many human aretefacts, the termites, which are known to have attacked and damaged human crania in ancient Egyptian graves. It is by no means unlikely that the Indian insect-ravagers may have done the same, and have annihilated the carvings and drawings made by the old people in this country on bone and ivory . . . . It is, I think, far from improbable that other caves than the Billa Surgam and Yerra Zari Gabbi groups, may exist in the great limestone

---

[1] *op. cit.* p. 188–9.

regions of the Cuddapah and Kurnool systems and their more westerly equivalents of Kaḷadgi and Bhīma series. Search should be made all over those limestone areas for caves that were unknown to the geological surveyors, for they had to get over such large tracts of country at great speed, that they might easily have missed caves in thickly jungled valleys, and many important caves may be unknown to the local natives. Caves may be hidden to a strange extent, by the falling in of the rocks over their entrance or mouth. That the old people might have possessed pigments, wherewith to produce coloured paintings if they desired to do so, is a well-known fact, and in several places many varieties of coloured clays and ochres occur in large quantities. A very interesting example of such a site occurs along the west boundary of the Dharwar rocks, which are exposed in the scarp of Raman Drug Hill, in Bellary district. The series of clay schists here met with contains examples of red of several shades, green, dark and light, blackish and other intermediate tints."

RELIGION

That palæolithic man did not indulge in dreams about post-mortem states of existence of the soul may be inferred from the lack of palæolithic graves. But as man is, besides a tool-making, a religious animal, we may well believe that palæolithic man had evolved rites of sacrifice to guardian spirits. The lowest stratum of religious life in each Indian village to-day is concerned with the propitiation by bloody sacrifice of the goddess or god, who, residing in the boundary of the village, protects the men and animals who live therein. The personality of these goddesses and gods is of the flimsiest kind and we may well believe that they came down from palæolithic times, because their chief weapon, and often the physical representative of the supernatural being, is but a mace. These village deities are more often goddesses than gods. This indicates that the family organization which grew in the later palæological sub-periods was matriarchal in character, such as is also proved by the well-known relics of the matriarchate in several corners of modern India. In later times, when Agama theology systematized the Indian pantheon, these innumerable local goddesses were made the attendants or manifestations of the great mother-goddess, Kali, worshipped so largely in India to-day, especially in those parts of the country where the influence of the Vedic religion did not become paramount.

Other traces of the more elaborate rites of the Nishāda Agê are to be found in the human sacrifices, called Meriah, associated sometimes with the use of stone tools, which were prevalent among the modern Nishādas (loosely called Khonds in the Vizagapatam and Ganjām agency tracts), till the British Government put a stop to it in the middle of the last century. Human sacrifice (*Naramedhayāgam*) was common in the Vedic Age ; most elaborate descriptions of the rite are found in the *Yajurveda Samhitas, Yajurveda Brāhmaṇas*, the *Sānkhāyana* and the *Vaitāna Sūtras*. The rite includes such repulsive incidents as the introduction of the *Śepas* of the *Medha* into the *Yoni* of the *Yajamāna*'s chief wife, (*mahishi svayamevāśvaśiśnam ākṛishya svayonau sthāpayati*) accompanied by the recitation of long strings of mantras. In fact one mantra[1] shows that there was a competition among the queens as to who was to receive this high honour. The texts related to the *Purushamedha* contemplate in some places an actual human sacrifice and in others a symbolic one. Apparently the human sacrifice was so ancient that it had become too holy to be given up, and, later, on account of the growing moral sense of the more refined classes, was converted into a symbolic sacrifice. In passing I may remark that the famous mantra beginning with *Udirshva āri*, now used in funeral ceremonies and hence interpreted to refer to widow re-marriage, has really no such implication, because its proper use is in connection with the horse or the human sacrifice, where the queen was called upon by means of this mantra to rise from the side of the sacrificial victim, after the above-described rite was over, and rejoin her living husband who was waiting for her.

Human sacrifices are not quite extinct to-day notwithstanding the spread of *Pax Britannica;* they are also continued vicariously in the religio-magical practices in which parts of a man's body, like hairs, nails, etc., are offered. Besides human sacrifices, elaborate buffalo sacrifices take place to-day in the heart of the forest. To these none but the tribesmen are admitted; yet it is known that as in the greater vedic sacrifices (of which corresponding buffalo sacrifices of the Palæolithic Age were prototypes) a large number of animals were killed, their flesh boiled and offered to the gods. Buffalo sacrifices on a similar scale are referred to in the *Rig Veda*. Agni dressed for Indra, to enable him to kill

---

[1] *Vājasaneya Samhita*, xxiii, 18.

Vritra, the flesh of three hundred buffaloes and, to help to swallow it, prepared three lakes of Soma juice.[1] Similarly the consumption of buffalo flesh in the sacrifices of the Savaras above referred to, is accompanied by large potations of spirits distilled from the *moa* flower (instead of which toddy derived from the palm was probably used in the Stone Age); eating, drinking and indecent orgies still form a part of these secret ceremonies in the Ganjām district. These, as well as daubing the face with red ochre, so prominent a feature of Kāli worship even to-day, have come down from palæolithic times, with this difference, that, whereas flesh is now cooked in pots, in old times they roasted it on open fires. The orgiastic accompaniments of the abnormal developments of religion, which, as every one knows, prevail secretly to-day in various parts of India, have also their roots in the orgies of palæolithic man.

ANTIQUITY OF MAN

When did man first arise? Geologists tell us that in the far off past a Mediterranean Ocean spread across North India and China and separated the Old World into a northern and southern hemisphere; that then there was land connection between India and Africa on one side, and India and Australia and thence up to South America on the other; that the surface of the Deccan plateau then split and out poured from the bowels of the earth molten lava which spread over 500,000 miles of India's surface and formed the rock called Deccan Trap; and that then the Himalayas rose by successive movements from the Mediterranean Ocean which soon dried up. Was man a wonder-struck witness of this "Nature's last great phenomenon," as an Indian geologist has called it? When the Vedic rishis spoken of *sindhu samudram*, the ocean of the Sindhu, had they a recollection, however vague, of an ancient legendary tradition of the North Indian Ocean? When the rishis sang *idam vishṇur vichakrame tredha nidadhe padam samūḷham asya pāmsure triṇi padā vichakrame vishṇur gopāh adābhyah*,[2] "Vishnu strode over this, in three places he planted his step: (all) was enveloped in his dust, Vishnu, the unconquerable preserver, strode three steps," and, *Vishṇur nu kam viryāṇi pravocham yaḥ pārthivāni vimame rajāmsi yo askabhāyad uttaraṃ sadhasthaṃ vichakramānas tredha urugāyaḥ pratad vishṇuḥ stavate viryeṇa mṛigo na bhimaḥ kucharo girishṭhāh yasyorushu tṛishu vikramaṇeshu adhikshiyanti bhuvanāni*

[1] *R.V.*, v, 29-7-8.

[2] *R.V.* i., 22-17-18.

viśvā pra vishṇave śūsham etu manma girikshite urūgāyāya vrishṇe yaḥ idam dirgham prayataṃ sadhasthaṃ eko.vimame tribhir it padhebhiḥ [1]
"I declare the heroic deeds of Vishnu who traversed the mundane regions, who established the upper sphere, striding thrice, the wide-stepping; therefore is Vishnu celebrated for his heroism, terrible like a wild beast, destructive, abiding in the mountains, he, within whose three vast paces, all the worlds abide; let my inspiriting hymn proceed to Vishnu, the dweller in the mountains, the wide-stepping, the vigorous, who alone travelled with three steps this wide, extensive firmament," was this an anthromorphical description of the gradual rising of the Himalyan chain to its present height? The association of Vishnu with mountains, implied in the expressions *girishṭhāh, girikshite,* abiding in the mountains, dweller in the mountains, and phrases like *viryena mrigo na bhima,* terrible like a wild beast, so different from the later description of the same being as always full of grace and sleeping on the Ocean of Milk, except when he sends rays of his infinite potency to save the world from wicked oppressors, tempts me to suggest this idea. But the questions I have raised above cannot be answered at present. Certain geologists imagine that it counts for scientific righteousness to be over-modest in their calculations of the lengths of geological periods and will grudgingly allow man but a beggarly hundred thousand years of earthly life so far. If this estimate is correct, the above questions have to be answered in the negative. But they can be answered in the affirmative if the other estimate is true, that man's life on this planet has extended over many millions of years. That the latter estimate is nearer the truth is indicated by the peculiar surface lustre acquired by certain palæoliths, called, "aeonic tinting," by Prof. Flinders Petrie. The tinting of the earlier of these tools ranges in shade from the dark mahogany brown to a light chestnut brown and the later ones show a streaky coloration of black and white or a dense blue or white. The former are believed to have been subjected by natural agencies "to some solvent which made their surfaces white and absorbent, and that afterwards they were immersed in some material which permanently stained their surfaces."[2] This process required exposure for a prolonged period on a land-surface and then burial in certain soils for another long period of time.

---

[1] *R.V.* i., 154, 1–3.
[2] J. Reid Moir, *Science Progress* for October 1925, pp. 248–9.

Two palæolithic tools have been discovered in direct association with the bones of extinct animals—one in the gravels of the Narmadā valley, and the other, of the upper Godāvarī valley. "The former is a beautifully worked boucher and the latter a worked flake. It has been stated that the formation of the gravels in which these instruments were discovered may have commenced some 400,000 years ago."[1] Another fact that indicates the very long antiquity of the Palæolithic Age is thus reported by Foote:—"Typical palæoliths were deposited by flood action in a bed of coarse shingle (in Gujerat) over which more than 50 feet of other alluvial materials were deposited by the action of the river (Sabarmatī), and over this again nearly 200 feet in thickness of blown loess was heaped by the westerly winds from the Gulf of Cambay and the Rann of Cutch."[2] These facts show that a hundred thousand years as the age of man on the earth is far too modest an estimate.

DENSITY OF POPULATION

The map of palæolithic finds shows that in the palæolithic times India was not densely populated. A nomad life is not favourable to the growth of a large population. Infant mortality among wandering races of the primitive times when man was but the slave of nature must have been heavy. Moreover, till iron tools were made, the forests of India could not have been fully cleared, and without such a clearing a dense population could not have arisen. Moreover, the localities where palæolithic men could flourish were limited by the distribution of the rocks which yielded materials suitable for their implements. Hence it is probable that palæolithians did not densely inhabit the country.

---

[1] J. C. Brown, *op. cit.*, p. 2. [2] *op. cit.*, p. 15.

CHAPTER II

THE NEW STONE AGE

The Lithic Age in Europe was frequently broken by intrusions of glacial ice as well as by invasions of people from Africa and Asia. Hence anthropologists have evolved the theory of a hiatus between the Palæolithic and the Neolithic Age. In India Foote has noticed in one place on the banks of the Sabarmatī River a great thickness of alluvial deposits and blown sand between a site where he found palæolithic tools and the next one where neolithic people had left their traces.[1] This can but prove the great length of the Old Stone Epoch and not necessarily indicate a hiatus between it and the next one. Throughout South India there is no geological or other indication of catastrophic phenomena when the Palæolithic Age ended; in several places palæolithic settlements shade off gradually into neolithic ones. Hence it is safer to conclude that the Neolithic Epoch came as a result of gradual evolution from the preceding age. The substitution of trap-rock for quartzite, the acquisition of the skill to polish the tools made with trap-rock till they became extraordinarily smooth to the touch, the domestication of the wild dog, and the cultivation of the wild rice led to the peaceful evolution of the epoch of new stone tools from that of the older rough implements, the settled life of the neolithians from the nomad life of the palæolithians.

DOMESTICATION OF ANIMALS

The first great step man took in the conquest of nature was the domestication of animals. The dog was perhaps the first animal to be tamed. The wild dog watches from a safe distance the hunting expeditions of the lion and the tiger, and, after these beasts of prey have gorged themselves with the meat of the animals they have killed, he feeds on what is left. He must have similarly followed early human hunters, who easily discerned his usefulness for the chase and gradually domesticated him. The next animals to be tamed were the goat, the sheep, the cow, the ox, and the buffalo. The goat and the sheep do not require the help of man in the matter of grazing; they but require thin forests where they could range without fear of wolves and tigers

[1] *op. cit.*, pp. 15–16.

and eat everything in the form of foliage, right up along rugged pathways to the giddiest heights. The cow and the buffalo require wide-stretching grass-land, and the buffalo, pools of muddy water besides, to wallow in; these men had to provide for them. The domestication of the animals led to the development of the pastoral stage of life. Nomad life passed away and was succeeded by a semi-settled life in communities. Pastoral man had to change his habitat only when the grass-fields near became incapable of supporting his herds. This semi-nomad life led to the formation of joint-tribal life, the development of the patriarchate, and later, of the joint-family system. Herds constantly tend to multiply and require larger and larger fields of grass to graze on; the owner of the herd tends to grow richer and richer; he soon becomes the influential head of the clan and the king-priest of his tribe. Grass-land cannot be partitioned as easily as crop-land can be, among the many heirs of a patriarch; for a rice-field, however small, can support a small family, but grass-land, divided into small plots is unfit for the grazing of the ever-increasing herd of cattle. Hence the pastoral stage of human evolution promoted the growth of the joint-family system, which is still one of the characteristic features of Indian life.

The fact that kingship was evolved in the pastoral stage is enshrined in the Tamil language. The word for a king belonging to the earliest stratum of that language is *Kō*, *Kōn*, or *Kōnār* (கோ, கோன், கோனார்). From this word is derived the word *Kōṭṭai* (கோட்டை), the residence of the *Kō*, the royal house; and since from early times the palaces of kings were fortified by mud walls, *Kōṭṭai* has come to mean a fort. The word *Kōn* still retains in Tamil usage its original significance and is still used to indicate the caste of the cowherd and the profession of the herdsman. This proves that kingship came into existence during the semi-nomad conditions of pastoral life. The oft-recurring necessity of shifting the settlements of pastoral people, whenever the grass-fields round a settlement became exhausted, probably necessitated the organization of the tribe under the government of a leader.

THE DOMESTICATION OF PLANTS

Not very much later man learnt to raise food crops. The chief plants which passed from the wild to the cultivated state under the hands of the Indians of the Lithic Age were rice and millets, pulses of several kinds, and fruits, the chief of which were the plantain and the mango. The raising of these crops involved the classification of land into the "good crop land" (நன்செய் நிலம்) where rice was raised, and the "bad crop land" (புன்செய் நிலம்) where the rest were cultivated, "good" and "bad" in these phrases meaning "superior" and "inferior." The former cultivation required the conveyance of water during the season of floods in channels; and the latter necessitated the invention of water-lifts with leather buckets, the motive power being man walking up and down on wooden levers (ஏற்றம்), or animals that walked up and down inclined surfaces (கபிலை). The raising of rice developed the extraordinary patience for which the Indian ryot is noted. The plantain was raised, not from seed, but from shoots from its tuber for such a long time that the plant has forgotten to produce seeds.

Agriculture meant a more settled life and the development of subsidiary occupations, especially the trade of the carpenter who made wooden ploughs and other tools needed for weeding and levelling the ground, besides crude carts for removing agricultural produce to the huts where the people lived.

THE FIVE RACES

Other modes of life developed apace as a reaction to other forms of physical environment. The earliest stratum of the Tamil language contains words which name five natural divisions of inhabited land and the occupations that grew in each division. They are the *neydal* (நெய்தல்), the littoral region, the *marudam* (மருதம்), the plough-land, the *mullai* (முல்லை), the forest land, the *kuṛinji* (குறிஞ்சி), the hilly country, and the *pālai* (பாலை), the sandy desert. The people of the littoral region were called the *Paradar* (பரதர்), men of coastal culture, who were expert fishermen, sailors and divers. From Gujerat along the seashore south to Cape Comorin and thence north along the East Coast of India to the mouths of the Ganges, these people lived; it is from their modern descendants that lascars, who form the efficient and reliable crew of many British ships, are recruited. They were boat-builders from ancient days down to the present time; boat-carpentry has remained distinct from the timber-work needed for house-building and the making of carts and household furniture and tools; so much so that the boat-carpenter belongs to a distinct caste, called in the Telugu country *Oḍa-Baliji*, allied to that of fisherfolk, and regarded as much inferior in social status to the house-carpenter.

These people built boats, canoes, catamarans and coracles called *doṇi* (தோணி), wicker-work boats shaped like a basket and covered with hide, such as ply on rivers to this day. They not only crossed rivers by means of them, but on these frail vessels they ventured far into the "black" sea, and in later times became the carriers of the articles which India exported to foreign countries. They also dived for pearls and oyster-shells; for from ancient times Indians loved to deck their persons and decorate their cattle and their carts with pearl or mother-of-pearl. In the ploughland lived the *Veḷḷālas* (வெள்ளாளர்), the rulers of the flood, as their name indicates, who learned to convey the river-floods by channels to their fields. The Veḷḷāḷars were the most civilized of the neolithic people; among them rose the lords of the land, called the *Vēḷir* (வேளிர்), who formed the landed aristocracy and the patrons of poets of later times. In districts far from the river-valleys lived the *Kārāḷars* (காராளர்), the rulers of the clouds, who learnt to conserve the gift of the clouds in tanks and wells and lift the water therefrom and take it to their fields. These people raised the millets and the pulses, which when added to rice and milk become a perfect dietary.

In the *mullai* region between the riverain and the mountainous country dwelt the *Iḍaiyars* (இடையர்), men of the intermediate region, also called *Ayar* (ஆயர்), herdsmen. The leisurely occupation of tending cattle and sheep led to the development of music and dancing among the herdsmen. Even to-day these people are well known to lead a life full of mirth and jollity. Religious dances are very prevalent among the men and women of this caste. The men of the hilly country were called the *Kuṛavar* (குறவர்), and those of the desert region, the *Maṛavar* (மறவர்). These were hunters and nomads, the link between palæolithic and neolithic people. This ancient five-fold classification of men according to natural regions and the life which the environment imposes on people, is a splendid anticipation by the ancient Tamils of modern anthropo-geographical doctrines, which form much sounder anthropology than the division of men into races, which is being rapidly abandoned, because no unalterable characteristics which separate race from race really exist.

In the Vedas occurs the phrase *Pañcha janāḥ*, the five tribes. The commentators have not been able to give a satisfactory explanation of this phrase. Apparently the five tribes included all the people of India. The suggestion is worth considering whether by the *Pañcha janāḥ* is not meant the five classes of people above described, who constitute the people of India, as subdivided into the inhabitants of the five natural regions of the country.

DENSITY OF NEOLITHIC POPULATION

The neolithic folk rapidly increased in numbers and spread throughout the country, as is proved by the wide occurrence of tools of the New Stone Age. "Neolithic implements are distributed over a large part of Southern India, especially in the districts of Salem, Anantapur, Kurnool and Bellary, and they are common in Hyderabad. They occur all along the ranges which border the Gangetic Plains in the South, and are very prevalent in Bundelkhand, in certain parts of the United Provinces and in the northern districts of the Central Provinces. Many examples have been obtained in Gujerat, but the vast area which lies between it and the southern parts of the Bombay Presidency does not appear to have been examined yet. Recorded instances of their occurrence in the Punjab, Rajputana, and Sind (with the exception of the famous cores and flakes from Rohri on the Indus) are rare, but the prehistoric antiquities of these provinces have not received much attention. A few finds have been reported from the Gangetic alluvium, from the Assam Valley, and from the Naga hills. Though of extreme rarity in the flatter parts of Bengal, they are to be found in the highlands of this province and in Behar."[1] The great increase of population in India in neolithic times is also shown by the large number of tools of this age which have been picked up. "To speak of celts and kindred implements only, my collection contains over 1,000 specimens; and reckoning at a rough estimate those broken specimens left behind in the many old neolithic sites I visited, several thousand specimens must have been handled by me alone, to say nothing of those collected by other observers and preserved in other collections."[2] The population of the country increased rapidly when the culture of the people advanced in many directions.

CLEARING OF FORESTS

To enable this rapid increase of population the forests of old India had to be cleared. This was done chiefly by means of fire either spontaneously arisen or artificially lighted; the very thick forests of the Indo-Gangetic plain could not have been obliterated except by the help of fire persisting for a long time, and is referred

[1] Brown, *op. cit.*, p. 3. [2] Foote, *op. cit.*, p. 17.

to frequently in the Vedic hymns. In *R. V.* i. 65, 4 it is said *Ibhyān na rāja vanāni atti*, "as a king eats the rich (so he) eats the woods." A mantra describes the course of Agni in the woods as follows:—"Urged by the wind he spreads through dry wood as he lists, armed with his tongue for sickles, with a mighty roar. Black is thy path, Agni, changeless with glittering waves, when like a bull thou rushest eager to the trees, with teeth of flame, wind-driven; through the wood he speeds triumphant like a bull among the herd of cows, with bright strength roaming to the everlasting air; things fixed, things moving, quake before him as he flies."[1] Another says, "Like water down the chariotways, he roareth. On his black path he shines in burning beauty marked as it were the heaven that shines through vapour. Abroad, consuming the broad earth he wanders, free roaming like an ox without a herdsman—Agni refulgent, burning up the bushes, with blackened lines, as though the earth he seasoned."[2]

The Age of the Vedas was posterior to the Neolithic Age we are now considering. But the custom of destroying forests and making their sites fit for human settlements and for the pursuit of agriculture by the employment of forest conflagration, begun in the neolithic times, persisted through the Age of the Vedic mantras. Even in the age of Sri Rāma which was the latter half of the Vedic Age, the Daṇḍakāraṇyam extended almost to the confines of the kingdom of Ayodhya and had not been purified by Agni and converted into land fit to be occupied by Aryas.

NEOLITHIC TOOLS

The tools of the Neolithic Age were of far greater variety than those of the previous epoch. Twelve types of celts with sides of different shapes, six types of chisels,—square, triangular, etc.,—three of hammers, two of adzes, anvils, corn-crushers, cylinders, discs, anvils, hammer-stones, hones, mace-heads, mealing places on rocks *in situ*, two types of mealing stones, two of mealing troughs, mortars, mullers (for grinding powders on slab), net-sinkers, pestles, pivot-stones, pounders, polishing grooves, slabs for grinding, slick-stones (used to put a gloss upon the surface of cloth while still on the loom), stone vessels, vessels of steatite, tally-stones, thumb-stones (made to fit the hand and used for flaking), whetstones, palettes for rouge, pencils of steatite, phalli, besides beads of many

---

[1] *R.V.* i. 52–55.

[2] *R.V.* ii. 4, 6, 7, as translated by Griffith.

types, buttons, human and animal figurines, marbles (toys), pendants, and fire-drills—all of polished stones—have been so far discovered. Of unpolished artefacts we have rough anvils, three types of arrow-heads, bone-splitters, two types of burins, six types of cores, flakers, knives, lance-heads, lancets, mallets, potting stone for potters, saws, scalpels, three types of scrapers, sling-stones, spokeshaves, and wedges, as also selected stones of many kinds for various purposes. This long list excludes the wooden tools of which they must have had a very large variety and which have not survived.

Neolithic men made their polished tools of trap-rock; it is tougher and more tenacious than quartzite and is capable of being well polished. As their palæolithic ancestors selected individual large pebbles which they could convert into shapely tools with the minimum of chipping, so too the neolithic tool-makers were keen to save themselves labour. They "did not, except possibly in very rare cases, make their implements out of large pieces of freshly broken rock, but sought about on the trap dykes whence they procured their work material, for fragments of rock of suitable size and shape formed by convenient disposition of the joint planes, or shrinkage cracks set up in all igneous rocks when cooling from a highly heated condition. Such suitably shaped fragments of rocks were of very great assistance to the stone-chippers as they enabled them to form their several implements with very much less labour than if they had had to reduce large pieces of freshly broken rock to the comparatively small size of the axes, adzes, and hammers in general demand by their non-toolmaking neighbours."[1]

Mr. Foote examined a celt factory on the Kapgaḷḷu or "Peacock's hill" near Bellary. "The castellated summit of the Kupgal offered to its inhabitants several fine rock shelters of which they availed themselves gladly. One reason and probably the principal one for the special attraction of the celt makers to the Kupgal was the existence of a great dyke of dioritic traps which traverses the hill axially in a N. W. by W. direction. This dyke furnished the stone workers with an inexhaustible supply of excellent material of two sorts, the coarse black diorite and the fine-grained pale greeny-grey to drab trap which occurs in lenticular masses, often of larger size, included in the great diorite dyke . . . The celts and other polished implements are met

[1] Foote, *op. cit.*, pp. 59–60.

with in different stages of manufacture . . . (First the implement) was chipped into form roughly . . . (It was) advanced a stage by 'pecking,' that is, breaking down the angles of the different chippings with a sharp pointed instrument with the objects of decreasing very greatly the quantity of material which would have to be removed by grinding . . . (Then the implement was) ground and all excessive roughness removed . . . (Then) the ground surface was polished."[1]

In Mr. Longhurst's Annual Report of the Archæological Department, Southern Circle, Madras, for 1914-15, p. 39, is given this account of the manufacture of stone implements of neolithic times. "To the South and East of Demaketiapalle, a small village situated eleven miles to the east of Hindupur railway station in the Anantapur District of the Madras Presidency are a number of small rocky hills, more or less connected together and which rise abruptly from the plains. Running along the crest (of one of the hills) is an outcrop of black trap, which, when viewed from a distance resembles the ruins of a fort-wall . . . Most of the boulders are not complete, as almost all of them show signs of having been struck with stone hammers in order to produce the flakes required for working up into finished celts. Hundreds of flakes and partly made stone implements, together with a quantity of stone hammers, may be found lying around the bases of these boulders, the latter showing unmistakable signs of being the original blocks from which the flakes were struck. In some cases I was able to replace the flakes on the very blocks from which they were struck and thus the first process of the manufacture of a stone celt became apparent, so much so, that I was able to produce a number of stone flakes . . . by simply picking up a stone hammer and bringing it down with a good smart blow on the crown of one of the dome-shaped boulders. This part of the making of a stone implement is simple enough and does not require any practice, a stone hammer and a strong arm is all that is required. But the trimming of the edges of the flakes and the working of it up into an implement or weapon is a very different matter and a very difficult one. Judging from the number of partly finished celts lying on the ground, all of which were broken and useless as implements or weapons, it would appear that for every finished celt made, dozens of failures must have occurred. The finishing of the edges of the flakes must

[1] Foote, *op. cit.*, pp. 84-85.

have been done by pressure and not with the hammer. I tried this myself and found that the use of the hammer for this work invariably broke the flake, but I was successful in trimming the edges by pressure applied by the aid of another stone."

Other implements such as mealing stones, hammer-stones, flakers, etc., were made of various other materials such as granite, gneiss, hæmatite, quartzite, and grits of the Dharwar and Gondwana systems. Besides these, have been discovered in large numbers pygmy flints, "which are found in great profusion among the offshoots of the Vindhyans in the United Provinces, Rewah and Baghelkhand . . . together with the cores from which they are derived, and are of chert, agate, jasper and carnelian often of beautiful tints. They have been obtained from the open surface of the ground, from under earthy deposits on the floors of rocky shelters and caves, and from tumuli which also contained bones and pottery."[1]

Besides stone tools there have been found in neolithic sites numerous selected stones. "By the term selected stones are meant stones foreign to the locality in which they were found and which were brought there intentionally by human agency to be utilized in the preparation of some special implements. In many cases these selected stones were procured in some way or other from far distant places, and getting them must have involved considerable labour and travel on the part of the neolithic people."[2] The principal selected stones were chert, agate, jasper and chalcedony. "Under the head of selected stones might be included the material frequently brought from distant places for the manufacture of corn-crushers, mealing-stones and hammer-stones of various types."[3] Their general great size and weight show that they were transported on carts. They are quite handsome and remarkable for size. The use of these different varieties of selected stones implies the prevalence of an extensive system of barter and probably the development of a special caste devoted to the work.

DWELLINGS

No neolithic houses have been noted so far. Many houses were probably habitations of straw, e.g., of the great millet *Holcus sorghum*, or plaited twigs which, when abandoned, quickly crumbled to dust and left nothing to indicate that they once existed

[1] J. C. Brown, *op. cit.*, pp. 6-7. [2] Foote, *op. cit.*, p. 26. [3] *ib.* p. 27.

there. Others were built of wattle and clay, topped with bamboo or palm rafters, the upper ends of which were held together by being inserted into a broken pot, and covered with a thatch of coconut or palmyra leaves like the huts of the poor nowadays. The hemispherical roofs of huts, surmounted by a pot, became the prototype of the dome and *Kalaśam* of temples. Earthenware roofing tiles were not in use in neolithic times. There is no proper word for it in Tamil, the word *Odu* being a metaphorical extension from its original meaning of "shell" to shell-like thin roof-tiles. "Even mud-built huts leave no traces of themselves when in exposed positions, but are absolutely destroyed and washed away by the violent rains of the two monsoons and the yet more furious downpours which accompany some of the hot-weather thunderstorms."[1] The houses of tribal chiefs were built of timber of which there was a practically inexhaustible supply in ancient India; and as timber houses cannot survive the action of Indian weather conditions for more than a century or two, no traces of neolithic timber houses can be found now. But the practice of building houses of timber survived to the seventh century as testified to by Yuan Chwang and is not unknown even now in corners remote from the influence of changing fashion, like Travancore or Cashmere. In the hilly country, where tribal wars were frequent, the people lived on fortified hills. "The Deccan-Hill forts all rise abruptly out of the plain and command the cultivable tract around their foot, which in most cases is a black soil flat. On the larger hills the inhabitants had room for their habitations on the less steep part of the slopes, where there were frequently spaces free from rock on which they could conveniently build their houses. These spaces or terraces which are real linchets are often held up at their lower extremities by revetments of rough stones. They vary much in size, but are mostly small and frequently near the summit. Many of the hills are naturally castellated, the granite rocks being conveniently jointed by great vertical and by approximately horizontal joint planes which have caused the hills to be weathered into their characteristic shapes. The natural castellation of the hills was taken advantage of by the old stone-folk in many cases and improved upon here and there by the building of rough walls to stop passages which were inconvenient to the dwellers on the hills. These systems of vertical and very highly inclined joint-fissures

---

[1] Foote, *op. cit.*, p. 87.

have in many cases led to the formation of large and small rock shelters which must have afforded the hill dwellers great protection against both sun and rain. . . In no cases did I observe the castellated hills to be surrounded with circuit walls near their base but they may very likely have been enclosed by a thick hedge of thorny character, a true Zareba. . . In some cases the disposition of the summit blocks gave rise to the formation of small but valuable cisterns which would hold rain water in some quantity in very sheltered positions. An excellent example of this is yet to be seen on the summit of the fort hill at Bellary. These which did not dry up by mere evaporation between the rains of the two monsoons, were beyond the reach of the enemies' arrows. . . On many of the hills small tanks had been constructed in convenient corners."[1]

POTTERY

Many relics of pottery have been found in neolithic settlements, in the district of Anantapur, Cuddapah, Kurnool, Tinnevelly, Salem, Pudukottah, Trichinopoly and Bellary, and in Mysore, Hyderabad, Baroda, Kathiawar, Baluchistan and other regions. It is probable that at first kilns were not constructed for burning the earthenware but they were burnt in open fires; "a strong argument in favour of this idea is provided by the appearance of many good vessels which are black at the top, but pass down into red. The black part is imperfectly burnt and the red, if a bright red, thoroughly well burnt."[2] The types of pottery may be classified "as plain and decorated according to their general surfaces irrespective of shape and colour. In the plain group we see four sub-groups. a. rough, b. smooth, c. polished, d. painted. The sub-groups of the decorated variety are three in number and may be described as a. impressed b. moulded, c. incised, of which the third is much the least common, though the two former were not so simple and easy to produce."[3] One distinguishing feature of the pottery is the fast colouring of its surface. I have unearthed from neolithic graves burial-urns several thousand years old, but yet the enamel looking as fresh as if it had been put on yesterday. Urns, vases, bowls, figurines, lotahs, chatties, hookas, (for smoking ganja), cups, circular dishes, hut-urns, saucers, spouted vessels, lamps, and libation-vessels, have been recovered from various neolithic settlements.

[1] Foote, *op. cit.*, pp. 27–28. [2] Foote, *op. cit.*, p. 195.
[3] Foote, *op. cit.*, p. 30.

As regards the moulding and casting of pottery Foote points out that "the preparations of earthenware structures, such as hut-urns and other angular forms, demands the pressing of the moistened clay into moulds. This process of moulding was one which had been discovered prior to the invention of the potters' wheel, and so had seemingly been the process of cast vessels, which consists of pouring thick 'slip' (i.e., semi-fluid clay) into a hollow mould, and allowing it to acquire a sufficient consistency to admit of its being removed from the mould without deforming it, before placing it in the kiln."[1]

OCCUPATIONS

The chief occupations of women were, as now, cooking and assisting men at their various occupations. Besides wooden ones of various kinds, women had plenty of earthenware culinary implements. The chief things they cooked were, as now, rice and curry, and cakes of rice meal and preparations of millets.

The large variety of polished stone tools that have been discovered in neolithic sites indicates that the men pursued numerous avocations. In fact the work of the menfolk was quite as varied as that which obtains now in Indian villages, especially those that have not been affected by commercial intercourse with the world outside India. The village life was self-contained and except for the stones used for the manufacture of tools, there was not much necessity for the barter of any particular article. In some respects the ancient village occupations were more varied than now. The wood-worker and the stone-worker were more in demand than at present; for they used more wooden tools than in the later Iron Age; and as all other tools were made of stone and well polished, the stone-worker plied his trade very much more extensively than now. Moreover, timber was very much more used than now in the construction of human habitations; hence the worker in wood was very much more in demand. And as Indians from ancient times insisted on every wooden tool and every bit of wood used for the construction of houses and carts being decorated with line-carving, the carpenter was very much in demand and his status in society fairly high. The high social status of the wood-worker persisted in the Vedic Age, when the Rathakāra, maker of chariots, was the companion of kings.

[1] *op. cit.*, p. 193.

Nature has fitted the greater portion of the Deccan plateau for the production of cotton; and the neolithic Indians early developed the art of weaving cotton cloth. For a very long time since, the Indian supplied cotton goods to the rest of the ancient world. The various tools needed for this manufacture, except those made of wood, have been discovered in neolithic sites; and the presence of slick-stones among others proves that the neolithic Indian liked his cloth to be made smooth by the use of this tool.¶ Besides cotton-weaving, weaving in wool was also practised. This was confined to the *Mullai* region, where the *Kuṟumbars*, a special class of herdsmen, tended a short variety of sheep called *Kuṟumbāḍu*, whose wool was fitted to be woven into the blankets called *Cumblies* (கம்பளி). This is the only article of woollen dress needed in India, and from the Neolithic Age down to our own days, the *Kuṟumbars* have specialized in its manufacture. They inhabit the region fitted to raise the *Kuṟumbāḍu*. Recent historical investigators have by a misunderstanding of certain Tamil traditions wrongly identified these Kurumbars with the Pallavas, who were Kshatriyas descended from the Parthian kings who acquired sway over several provinces in India in the half-millennium preceding the Christian Era and who, among others, helped to spread Arya culture in Tamil and Telugu India.

Many other occupations were pursued in neolithic times, corresponding to the various kinds of tools that have been discovered. Of these prominent mention may be made of the leather industry which served the needs of the house and the farm and in which were used the finely made scrapers and cutting and hammering tools made of trap-rock. The professions largely depended on the environment of the workers; the dairyman lived in the *Mullai* country, the fisherman in the *Neydal*, and the hunter in the *Kuṟiñji* and the *Pālai* tracts. Pastoral and agricultural occupations were intimately associated with each other; this is perhaps symbolized by the fact that Krishna, the God of the Cowherds, who spent his time dancing with the milk-maids and playing on the flute, the first musical instrument made by man and specially associated with pastoral life even to-day, and Balarāma, whose implement was the plough and was always intoxicated with liquor, were brothers.

Trade by barter was also developed. Otherwise we cannot account for the presence of chert in the environments of Madura, though chert does not occur *in situ* in the district.

DRESS AND DECORATION

As the cotton plant is a native of the Deccan, the neolithic people early learnt to weave cotton cloth; the hide dress and the bark dress of the earlier age were reserved for occasions of sanctity. The supply of cotton being plentiful, they wove pieces of cloth several yards long and wrapped them round their waists, and more especially round their heads, to protect them from the sun. Such is still the prevailing fashion of dress among the natives of the cotton-districts. They discovered vegetable dyes; the neolithic people had a delicate colour-perception. The dyes used at first were yellow, indigo, and red. The first is the colour of Vishnu, the second of Krishna, and the last of Siva. Woollen cloth was woven by the pastoral tribe of Kurumbas, even perhaps before cotton cloth was woven.

Neolithic people decorated themselves, besides, with beads and buttons, and bangles of shell and bone. These have been picked up in various neolithic settlements and are still worn profusely by the classes of people who have not shared in the cultural advancement of later times. Ornaments of shell and bone and beads are still used for decorating the much-beloved cow.

Neolithic ladies made themselves attractive by peculiar styles of hair-dressing. In the Salem district have been found certain red earthenware figurines of women. "The special interest attaching to these figures is due to the unique style of head-dress they show, namely, having their hair dressed in short ringlets all round the head and wearing high combs on the top. The finding of these little female figures with such an elaborate style of hair-dressing throws light upon the use of a neck-rest unearthed in an old Iron age site on the north (left) bank of the Cauvery river opposite to the town of Tiruma Kodlu Narsipur in Mysore and just below the Sangam, or junction, with the Kabbani or Kapilla River. The use of a neck-rest was essential if the women desired to preserve their curls intact when sleeping."[1] Near the Guntakal Junction in Anantapur was discovered a wooden comb, such as was used by neolithic ladies referred to above. "This comb escaped the greed of the white ants because imbedded in a layer of white ash, a substance they hate immensely as contact with it

---

[1] Foote, *op. cit.*, p. 61.

greatly disagrees with their soft moist bodies."[1] This comb was found in a neolithic site, wherefrom a valuable series of earthenware was also obtained.

CLASSES OF POPULATION

It is likely that the people became divided into numerous endogamous castes and these castes developed peculiar customs due to the professions they followed, the geographical influences of the districts in which they lived and worked, and the dialects they spoke. This subdivision into castes has nothing to do with the division of the people into four Varnas. The division into four Varnas is a later framework evolved with reference to the Vedic Yajña and imposed on a pre-existing classification into numerous castes, wherever and whenever the fire-rite spread. The many castes are ancient institutions; the four Varnas—a cross-division only—related to the fire-rite and more recent than the former.

ART

Nature puts on brilliantly coloured robes in tropical countries and this certainly stimulated the colour-perception of the neolithians. "The extent to which the neolithic people were interested in, and affected by, perception of colour is not easy to gauge, as few indications of their love of varying tints remain; still there are four facts from which inferences can be drawn. Firstly, the several tints they allowed their pottery to receive by varying the degree of firing they exposed the pots to. Secondly, the pigments they used to paint the different vessels the potters turned out, were shades of red, yellow, brown, and rarely orange and purplish grey. The third fact is the great fondness the old folk had for pistacite granite with its mixture of green and pink colours and for chrome gneiss with its delicate greenish white and green tints. In many cases, specimens of these two rocks must have been fetched from great distances, though they would have served no better than the common country rock for the making of mealing-stones and corn-crushers for which they were generally used. The fourth fact or seeming fact lies in the very pretty and often quite gay colours of many of the selected stones gathered by the old people from quite distant places, e.g., the pleasing colours of the cherts and agates they collected to convert into drill-head flakes, scrapers and strike-a-lights."[2] Moreover,

---

[1] *ib.* p. 12. [2] Foote, *op. cit.*, p. 23.

"the walls and roofs of the cave which yield pigmy flints, are sometimes covered with rough drawings in ruddle or hæmatite. Similar ones, illustrating hunting scenes, occur in the Kaimur Range, and it is believed from the primitive outlines of the depicted weapons that some of the drawings are of the neolithic age. Beautiful examples of this art have recently been found in caves near Raigarh in the extreme east of the Central Provinces Specimens of earthy red hæmatite, which have been rubbed down to produce a red colour wash, have been discovered at no less than thirteen neolithic sites in the Deccan, while the collection of the Indian Museum contains many specimens from the Hazaribagh district in Behar. Two small palettes for grinding down this material to produce rouge have been described from Bellary and from Maski in the Raichur doab."[1]

A few representations of natural objects on pottery have been met with. Such are leaf patterns, impressions on painted fillets in vessels representing leaves like those of *Emblica officinalis* (நெல்லி) the prototype of the much later Āmalaka shaped Kalaśams of Orissan temples, imitations of fruits, etc. "Very noteworthy as a good moulded imitation of a fruit is the side of a large melon bowl (found at Maski) . . . decorated with a fillet of rasp-berries outside below the lip . . . The bowl when entire must have been a distinctively handsome vessel."[2]

On the left bank of the river opposite to the town of Ham-pasagara in Bellary district Foote came across in a neolithic burial place a funeral vase of the shape of an elephantoid quadruped. Excepting the head and three or four small pieces of the body, the whole vase or urn was recovered.[3] But no prehistoric pottery made in the shapes of birds or with human figures painted thereon have been found. The artistic instincts of Indians did not work in the direction of reproducing the shapes of natural objects. Indian art has been not imitative, but decorative, in motive. It is an old Indian custom to decorate all wooden artefacts such as sills, pillars, cross-beams of carts, yokes, vessels and tools of all kinds (and after metal was discovered, all metal tools) with line-drawings representing the lotus and other flowers, fruits, leaves and creepers. A decorated chatty of neolithic times has been found "on the east side of the great mounds at Guḍivāḍa in the Kistna district. Besides other decoration, this great vessel, which was probably a grain store, shows a broad band of floral decoration of bold pattern

[1] J. C. Brown, *op. cit.*, p. 4. [2] Foote, *op. cit.*, p. 31.
[3] Foote, *op. cit.*, p. 185.

between two fillets of pinnate impressions."[1] Decorated bangles have been recovered in various places. Shell bangles show decorative carvings of various devices on their backs.[2] Others show "a raised fillet of right sloping barlets lying between two grooves."[3] The love of decoration of the person and the personal belongings has been, throughout the ages, the greatest expression of the artistic instincts of the Indian people. Indian ladies are, even today, fond of decorating the front of their houses with patterns in coloured powder, and the walls of their houses with elaborate designs in colour. These customs come down from the neolithic times, and hence the great attachment of our ladies to this form of art, which has acquired a sacred character in their eyes. A good example of pot-decoration by women is the "much-painted pot, polished outside but rough inside," the shoulder of which was found two miles above Babapur in Kathiawar. "The colour is applied in bands seven in number, of which one broad and two narrow bands are red, three bands are purple and one is pink."[4]

DISPOSAL OF THE DEAD

The neolithic people buried their dead. The best district for the study of the burial customs of neolithic man is the Pudukkottah State. The burial sites are so many that it appears the region round the modern town of Pudukkottah must have been occupied by man continuously from the Palaeolithic Age right up to modern times. A careful examination of the sites shows that dead men were buried in mud pits or placed in pots before burial. Most probably the poor were disposed of in the former fashion. The rich were given a grander burial. The dead man was placed in a sitting posture in an earthenware pot, the pot was then let into a pit and half filled with sand, and rice and other grains on a tray were placed before the dead man. His stone tools were also inserted at the sides of the pot. The foodstuffs and tools were no doubt intended for the use of the dead person in his post-mortem life, for the neolithians believed in the life of the spirit of man after death. Then more sand was poured into the pot till it was full and the pot covered with an earthenware lid. The pit was then filled in and a stone slab placed on it. Then more sand was poured and another stone slab, this time very large and oval in

[1] Foote, *op. cit*, p. 31.
[2] *ib.*, p. 149.
[3] *ib.*, p. 125.
[4] Foote, *op. cit.*, p. 149.

shape, was placed above the grave and upright stones about a cubit long planted all round the slab. Each site, containing several such graves, numbering two dozen or more of varying sizes, is surrounded and marked off from neighbouring sites, by a circular row of upright stones, and forms an ancient family vault. Miles and miles of such burial sites, generally near water-courses, have been observed by me in the Pudukkottah territory. Usually these sites are found in elevated places and are covered with a few feet of earth, so that it looks like a patch of dry land. By knocking the ground with a hammer, one could detect a hollow sound wherever a grave exists. The burial urns vary in size, the largest measuring 4 feet in height and 3 feet 6 inches in diameter in the broadest part. They are sometimes adorned with incised lines. The graves of the New Stone Age are oval in shape and those of the succeeding Iron Age oblong, often divided into two square compartments; they are lined with stone slabs and separated by a thin stone-slab wall with a hole in the centre. Tombs made of big blocks of stones called megalithic tombs, in a great variety of forms, occur in the central and southern parts of the peninsula. From the Bellary district alone, over two thousand have been recovered.[1] Officers of the Archæological Department have discovered megalithic tombs in the Coimbatore district. Oblong terra cotta sarcophagi standing on short legs have been found at Pallavaram, near Madras, and earthenware coffins in several neolithic sites. Hut-urns have been discovered in Salem and in Gujerat.

NEOLITHIC INDIA AND THE REST OF THE WORLD

"The type of megalithic tomb, so common in the Deccan, which has a small hole in one of the walls, is also distributed throughout Britain, France, Central Germany, Scandinavia, Sardinia, Syria, and the Caucasus. The cup-makings found on the stones of dolmens in some countries are not unknown in India. Recently examples have been found in Kashmir."[1] The investigations of Elliot Smith, Rivers and Percy show that the fashion of megalithic tombs spread from Egypt to India and other countries.[2] This means that there were world-wide movements of people in neolithic times. Such movements were attributed by Huntingdon in the *Pulse of Asia* to periodical droughts in several Asiatic countries,

---

[1] J. C. Brown, *op. cit.*, p. 7.
[2] Article on the *Aims of Ethnology* by Rivers in *Psyche*, Oct. 1922.

but they seem to have been inspired more by desire for gold, pearl, mother-of-pearl and precious metals like jade, and this indicates extensive commerce by means of barter in neolithic times.

Other evidences of extensive intercourse between India and the world outside it in the Neolithic Age exist. There is a remarkable resemblance between the terra cotta sarcophagi found at Pallavaram and "certain terra cotta coffins discovered near Baghdad, and also between the latter and the more highly developed and ornamental Etruscan terra cotta coffin-tombs."[1] Numerous legged vessels of the neolithic times resemble in shape some of the vessels found by Dr. Schliemann in the ruins of Troy. Foote found near the French Rocks near Mysore "part of a large chatty with two ornaments cuneiform in shape, with a small pap in each re-entering angle and a raised garland-like ring surrounding each cross."[2] This is evidently a *Swastika*, and it bears a strong resemblance to the Trojan type of Swastika. These facts negative the hasty assumptions of historians about the age-long isolation of India from the rest of the world and prove that in the Lithic Ages, as later, India had an active intimate intercourse, cultural and commercial, with the rest of Asia, with Africa and Europe.

LANGUAGE

Dialects of the same family of languages were spoken throughout India, except in the Vindhyan regions, in the Neolithic Age; and that is what has been called the Dravidian family. The distinction between the spoken dialects of North India, to which the name Gauḍian has been given by modern scholars and which have been held to be degenerations of Sanskrit or of Prakrit, and those of Southern India, to which the name Dravidian has been given, is, I hold, a distinction without a difference, except that the North Indian dialects have been very much more profoundly affected by Sanskrit than those of South India. The neolithians of North India spoke languages of their own which, I hold, were structurally allied to the so-called Dravidian family of languages and not to Sanskrit or to Prakrit. It is well known that the several Prakrits, of which we have specimens in dramatic and other literature, were artificial literary dialects used only in literature and restricted therein to the lower classes. They are allied to Sanskrit and totally different in structure from the actual spoken dialects of

---

[1] J. C. Brown, *op. cit.*, p. 7. [2] *op. cit.*, p. 73.

North India, such as are found in the inscriptions of Asoka. These dialects, as well as the so-called Gauḍian dialects now spoken in Northern India, from Punjabi down to Oriya, agree in grammatical structure with the so-called Dravidian dialects of South India. The family relationships of languages can best be ascertained not so much by similarities of their vocables but by an examination of the essential structure of the languages, by their schemes of accidence, of gender, number and cases of nouns and adjectives, of voice, mood, number, gender, tenses and other inflections of verbs, and of their essential syntactical structure—such as the order of words in sentences and the methods of formation of idioms. A comparative study of modern North Indian and South Indian dialects reveals the fact that their fundamental grammatical structure is so very much the same that it is possible to translate from one of these languages into any other by the simple process of the substitution of one word for another—a procedure absolutely impossible when translating from Sanskrit or English into any of the spoken dialects of ancient or modern India. English and Persian are dialects of the Indo-Germanic family of languages which have passed from the synthetic to the analytic stages but the dialects of Northern India are not synthetic languages in the analytic stage, but are essentially similar to the South Indian languages in their grammatical frame-work. It is a well-known conclusion of comparative philology that it is possible for a language to borrow almost all its vocabulary from another language, but its grammatical frame-work, dependent on the particular bent of mind of its speakers, cannot be altered by the influence of a foreign language; and the grammatical frame-work of all the spoken languages of India from Asokan days to our own has been the same. I hold therefore that all the spoken languages of India (perhaps including the Nishada dialects, too) are dialects of one family of languages—not the Indo-Germanic family—which may be called Pan-Indian and that they are *deśi* in essential structure, and therefore evolved in India in neolithic times, if not earlier.

The vocabulary of every Indian spoken dialect is partly Sanskritic and partly *deśi*, i.e., indigenous, non-Sanskritic. The large proportion of *deśi* words in every Indian dialect itself proves that all these dialects existed long before the Sanskrit language began to influence them; for it is inconceivable that a people who had the extraordinary wealth of Sanskrit vocabulary at their disposal could have borrowed words largely. The people of Northern India came very much more under the influence of Sanskrit than those of Southern India; hence many grammatical forms of Sanskrit have found a lodgment in their dialects; on this account people are misled into believing those dialects to be degenerations of the Sanskrit language. The fact of the matter is that from neolithic times the people of India spoke different dialects of one original family, which was not the Indo-European family.

Sanskrit came into prominence about five thousand years ago in Northern India. It appeared from the beginning not as an Indian vernacular, but as the handmaiden of the Arya fire-cult, a literary language, used as the vehicle of the aspirations of the rishis when they appealed to the gods to satisfy their longings in this world and the next. The Hindus have called it the language of the gods—*deva bhāshā*—and this apparently means that there is no evidence of its employment as a vernacular by common men in their ordinary secular life before it became the language of the mantras by means of which men spoke to the gods. The theory of evolution and the name *Samskrita*, the refined, have led men to believe that it must have been evolved from a previous *Prākrita* stage, when it perhaps served the ordinary humble purposes of every-day life. A German philologist of the middle of the nineteenth century was so fool-hardy as to invent the *ursprache* of the Indo-Germanic family of languages—the imaginary original Aryan tongue—and even to write some tales in that imaginary language, but this served but to excite the ridicule of linguists. Later students of the science of languages, inspired by the recent development of the science of phonology have attempted to reconstruct, though not the *ursprache*, but yet words and roots probably belonging to it. These are but interesting speculations, because there is no historical evidence of what the *ursprache* was like when it existed as a spoken dialect, as theory compels us to regard that it must have existed; limiting ourselves strictly to the available evidence, we can but say that the Vedic language, as we know it, could not have been a spoken dialect. "Some writers call the Vedic language the vernacular of the ancient people of the Punjab valley. This is not true, for there must have been various dialectical differences between the speeches of contiguous tribes as there is everywhere on the earth; and moreover the language of literature, all the world over, differs from the actual speech of men and women. It is but primitive ballads that are in the spoken idiom of any tribe, and the mantras are not simple ballads of love and war sung by a primitive people, but they are composed in an artificial style, full of archaisms and poetic constructions and complicated, well defined metrical forms, of which there are sixty in the Rig Veda Samhitā, and under the influence of a well developed literary convention. The extraordinary care with which the musical accent (*svara*) of the mantras was preserved in their recitation is another proof that the Vedic language was a sacred dialect and not a vernacular."[1] Dr. Macdonell calls the Vedic language a "caste-language", a "scholastic dialect of a class," "an artificially archaic dialect, handed down from one generation to the other within the class of priestly singers."[2] Hence it could not have been a vernacular nor have become the parent of the vernaculars of Northern India now spoken by the Brāhmana and the Chamār. The fact that the knowledge of Sanskrit was restricted to Aryāvartta, north of the Vindhyas, for several thousand years and did not influence the South Indian dialects, from the primitive Kui to the polished Tamil, which latter attained the position of a vehicle of literature, independent of Sanskrit influence, has led superficial enquirers into the belief that the northern dialects are Sanskritic and the southern dialects non-Sanskritic. On the contrary all the spoken dialects of modern India belong to one linguistic family, other than the Indo-Germanic family.

THE MYTH OF THE IMPORTATION OF THE SOUTH INDIAN LANGUAGES FROM OUTSIDE INDIA

Certain investigators assume that everything Indian must have been imported at some remote time from outside India. They hold that the speakers of primitive Tamil and other South Indian languages, to whom they give the name of the Dravidian race, must have settled in India from Central Asia. These theorists drag large bodies of ancient people along the map of Asia and Europe as easily as chessmen are shifted on the chess-board, and make them wander aimlessly from country to country, merely to support their baseless theories. It happens that certain words of the Brahui dialect of Baluchistan resemble certain Tamil words.

---

[1] P. T. Srinivasa Ayyangar's *Life in Ancient India in the Age of the Mantras*, p. 3.

[2] *Sanskrit Literature*, p. 2.

To explain this solitary fact, which is susceptible of various interpretations, they will have it that an ancient Dravidian race, evolved somewhere outside India in the Asiatic highlands, undertook a pilgrimage to India through its north-western gate, and reached the extreme south through strange and devious ways[1]. Foote constructs an itinerary for the wanderings of these peoples,[2] which is a specimen of perverse ingenuity without any historical evidence to support it. Surely the neolithians of India were not dumb animals, but spoke languages of their own. The simplest hypothesis under the circumstances is, as Tamil traditional history holds, that the Tamils and other allied peoples were indigenous and their languages were evolved where they are now spoken. A careful study of South Indian prehistoric antiquities *in situ* cannot lead to any other conclusion than that the passage of culture from stage to stage in ancient times was not a catastrophic change such as indicates the struggle of alien intruders with the pre-existing population but a peaceful course of evolution. An inspection of the map of neolithic India is enough to prove that the country was thickly populated by people of one homogeneous form of culture and that that people ought to have been autochthonous, as the Tamil people have always claimed to be, in the traditions recorded in their literature. In the most ancient layers of the Tamil language can be discovered, not only ample traces of neolithic culture, but also the birth of the iron-age culture that succeeded it.

THE BIRTH OF THE IRON AGE

Every one who has observed iron tools occurring in old neolithic village sites, who has seen with his eyes how stone celts are mixed with artefacts of the Early Iron Age and how the latest neolithic and earliest iron ages overlap, will endorse Foote's remark that "from the evidence afforded by several old sites in the Deccan and Mysore it is a very reasonable inference that the iron workers were the direct successors of the neolithic people."[3]

The discovery of fire was a happy accident of prehistoric times. While a big neolithic fire was lighted on a primitive hearth made of three blocks of iron-stone (which is abundant in Southern India), for boiling large quantities of meat for a tribal feast or a buffalo sacrifice to the tribal god, the fire developed enough heat to melt the iron ore and make the liquid metal flow out. It was soon

---

[1] Holdich, *Gates of India*, pp. 142-4. [2] *op. cit.*, p. 38-39.

[3] *op. cit.*, p. 3.

found that iron was a much better material for tools than stone; whence once this was realized, stone implements were superseded, except for ceremonial purposes, for which the ancient holy stone tools were continued to be used. The discovery of iron was soon followed by the discovery of gold, silver and copper. These metals were found and named long before any contact was made between the Arya fire-cult with its sacred language, Sanskrit, and the fireless (*anagniḥ*) cult of South India. The Vedic culture was not a lithic one but belonged to the age of metal tools. Before it arose in North India, Tamil was able, from its own resources, to invent names for the four metals of South India; iron was called *irūmbu* (இரும்பு, the earlier form being *irumu*), from the root *ir*, dark (also the base of *iruḷ*, இருள், darkness, *irā* or *iravu*, இரா, இரவு, night, etc.); copper was called *śembu*, (செம்பு), from *śem*, red; silver, *veḷḷi* (வெள்ளி), from *veḷ*, white; and gold, *pon* (பொன்) from *pol*, to shine. When the general idea of "metal," the lustrous mineral, was reached, *pon* became the general name of metal, and gold got several other names of which *tangam* (தங்கம்), the pure, never-tarnishing metal, was one. Tin and lead were introduced into Southern India from Northern India; hence their names, *tagaram* (தகரம்) and *iyam* (ஈயம், modified form of *sisam*) were borrowed from Sanskrit or Prakrit. These considerations support Foote's opinion that the iron industry of South India is of great antiquity, far greater indeed than that of Europe.[1] No one who has opened South Indian graves of the Stone Age and of the Early Iron Age and seen with his own eyes how the former shades off into the latter, can escape coming to the conclusion that iron was first discovered in South India. This also explains why ancient Indian blacksmiths became expert workers in iron and steel, and tools made of these materials were exported to Africa and Asia several thousand years ago, and why so late as in the fourth century B.C., Alexander of Macedon demanded from the Malavas one hundred tons of "white iron" (i.e., Indian steel, whose excellence was renowned throughout the ancient world) as a tribute, in preference to gold.

RELIGION

Siva is a hunter-god and numerous legends concerning him suggest palæolithic and early neolithic modes of life; hence his worship probably comes down from the lithic stage of development of human culture in India. Sanskrit grammarians have not

---

[1] Foote, *op. cit.*, p. 25.

been able to discover a satisfactory etymology for the name of this god. It has been suggested that the name is derived from the Tamil word for "red" (சிவ), because he is a red god and that the name Rudra, "the red one" is a Sanskrit translation of the Tamil name. Whether this derivation is sound or no, it is certain that the worship of Siva in the form of the phallus) existed in neolithic times, for phalli of stone and earthenware have been found among neolithic artefacts. "Among the interesting neolithic finds on the Shevaroy hills is a phallus, a small object of pale gneiss diminishing biconically and truncated with flat ends . . . It is of great interest as proving that the neolithic people had faith in the doctrine of male energy"[1] In later days when the Arya fire-rite rose, the Indra-cult, which was an important part of the fire-rite, came in conflict with the rival cult of those whom the rishis called the Śiśna Devas. *R. V.* vii. 21—5, addressed to Indra, says, "Neither demons impel us, Indra, nor, O Puissant, of a truth any evil spirits. The glorious (Indra), defies the hostile beings; let not those Siśna Devas approach our sacred ceremony." *R. V.* x. 99-3 speaking of Indra, says, "Proceeding to the conflict, and desiring to acquire them, he has gone to, and in hostile array besieged, inaccessible places, at the time, when, irresistible, slaying the *Śiśnadevas*, he by his craft conquered the riches of the city with a hundred gates." Yaska's explanation of the word as *Abrahmacharyāh*, the unchaste, and Sāyana's, as *Śiśnena Divyanti, Kriḍanti*, are inappropriate, as the context shows that a tribe following a rival cult is referred to. The *Sivas* are mentioned, in *R. V.* vii. 18, 7 as one of the tribes opposed to the Indra-worshipping Tritsus; the *Śiśnas* are referred to, in *R. V.* x. 27, 9 as advancing against Indra. These passages indicate the opposition of the worshippers of the phallus to the worshippers of Indra. The cult of the phallus was in ancient times, as it still continues to be, a "fireless" cult, and the Indra-cult, all but dead in modern India, a fire-cult The wars between the Aryas and the Dasyus, misunderstood by modern students to be due to a war of invasion, were but fights between two opposed cults. Hence the Śiśnadevas were Dasyus who opposed the worshippers of Indra-Agni. The Puranas contain many legends about the antagonism between Siva and the Vedic gods to whom sacrifice was offered through fire. However, before the end of the Vedic Age, there was a movement toward the reconciliation of these warring cults; the immediate result of which was that the

---

[1] Foote, *op. cit.*, p. 61.

cult of the phallus, under the name Skambha, was affiliated to the Vedic rites, and *A. V.* x. 7 was composed as a Vedic hymn celebrating the phallus; the remoter result of this movement is modern Hinduism which has made Siva, the Mahadeva, the greatest god of the Vedic pantheon.

Krishna is the deity of pastoral tribes, and his flute, the invention of the pastoral stage of culture. His *Rāsalila*, singing and dancing in the midst of young girls tending cattle, is an institution peculiar to people even now following pastoral avocations. Cowherds and cowherdesses are even to-day devotees of Krishna and celebrate his worship with ceremonials peculiar to themselves throughout India, different from the ways in which Krishna is worshipped by divisions of the population, that have reached a higher degree of culture than the pastoral. A comparison of the Krishna-cult as it obtains among milkmen and milkmaids with that which prevails among the more cultured Indians clearly shows that the former comes unaltered from lithic times and unaffected by conceptions derived from the life of the Krishna of the age of the Mahābhārata.

Modern scholars, while being unreasonably sceptical about the value of the historical chapters of the Puranas in the matter of re-constructing the dynastic history of the Vedic Age, still accept the legendary portions of the Puranas and regard the Krishna-cult as later than the time of the historical King of Dvārakā, who played such an important part in the drama of the Mahābhārata. That there was a Krishna earlier than the *avatāra* of a ray of Vishnu who figured in the great convulsion of the war between the Kauravas and the Pandavas, is indicated by Krishna being particularly described as *Devakiputra* in the Chāndogya Upanishad and that there was a Krishna and there were Krishnas, long before the Mahābhārata war, is proved by the quotations given below from the *Rig Veda*, which were composed long before that war, long before Veda Vyasa fixed the Vedic canon for all time. I have discussed this god in my *Life in Ancient India in the Age of the Mantras*[1] and I here reproduce that discussion:—"Another foe of Indra in the age of the mantras, was a god or deified hero of a tribe called the Kṛishṇas. Of him it is said, 'The fleet Kṛishṇa lived on the banks of the Amśumatī (Jumna) river with ten thousand troops. Indra of his own wisdom became cognizant of this loud-yelling chief. He destroyed the marauding host for the benefit of Arya men. Indra said, 'I have seen the

[1] pp. 131–2.

fleet Kṛishṇa. He is lurking in the hidden region near the Amśumatī like the sun in a cloud. O Maruts, I desire you to engage him in fight and to destroy him, the fleet Kṛishna then appeared shining on the banks of the Amśumatī. Indra took Brihaspati as his ally and destroyed the fleet and godless army.[1] Indra with Rijiśvā, son of Vidathī, killed the pregnant wives of Kṛishṇa.[2] Indra smote 50,000 Kṛishṇas as old age destroys the body.[3] European scholars have interpreted *Drapsah Kṛishṇah* in the first of these passages as the 'black drop' possibly because they believe that the Krishna-cult rose later; but there is absolutely no reason why beliefs on *a priori* grounds should override Indian tradition which makes Kṛishṇa one of seven Indra's demon-foes, he 'who never had met a rival' till Indra was born.[4] In fact the translation 'black drop' makes the whole passage meaningless. Krishṇa was the enemy of Indra throughout the whole course of the development of religion in India. The Puranas which certainly contain very old legends, many older than the Vedic age, describe many conflicts between Indra and Krishṇa, in one of which Kṛishṇa put an end to the worship of Indra on the banks of this very Jumna, among the tribes that lived in the woods near that river. The phrase 'fleet Kṛishṇa' vividly brings home to us that he was from early days the god of wandering pastoral tribes, probably called the Vṛishṇis—the *Ram* tribe. The antagonism of the Kṛishṇa-cult to the Indra-cult not only recurs constantly in the legends but a far off echo of it is heard even in the Bhagavad-Gīta where Kṛishṇa refers scornfully to the 'flowery words' of the 'fools' who delight in the Vedas, which as we know were born from the Indra-cult, and which Kṛishṇa advises his followers to reject because they bewilder the mind.[5] And Krishṇa, the god of the early Indian pastoral tribes, became the nucleus round which gathered other tales, possibly of human heroes, other cults, e.g., the Vāsudeva-cult of the Bhāgavatas, the Vishṇu-cult of the Vaishṇavas, till, to-day, Krishna-worship is the dominating religion of India and the Indra-cult practically dead. It is also interesting to note that notwithstanding the accretion of so many tales round the name of Kṛishṇa, it is the cowherd playing the flute to his cattle on the banks of the Jumna and sporting with the simple village maidens that still appeals to the mind of the Hindu."

---

[1] *R.V.* viii, 85-13-15.
[2] *Ib.* i, 101—1, ii, 20—7.
[3] *R.V.* iv, 16-13.
[4] *R.V.* viii, 85—16.
[5] ii, 42, 45, 46, 53.

The modern conception of Vishṇu seems to be the result of syncretism. (1) Vishnu, the terrible mountain-dweller, the god of some ancient hill-tribe, (2) Vishṇu, the wide-stepper, explained by Yāska as the Sun who steps from the eastern horizon to the zenith and from the zenith to the western horizon and whose name was probably derived from Tamil *Viṇ* the sky, (3) the Vedic Vishṇu, always described as *Yajño Vai, Vishṇuh*, the sacrificial victim of the gods, the Purusha who was cut up to form the universe, (4) Nārāyaṇa who is always sleeping on the Serpent Couch in the Ocean of Milk, whose first manifestation (*vyūha*) is Vāsudeva, the All, and whose working aspects are Brahmā the Creator, Vishṇu the Preserver, and Īśvara, the Destroyer, the three aspects being embodied in the three filaments of guṇas—*Rajas, Satva*, and *Tamas*, that are the first evolutes of *mūlaprakṛiti*, chaotic matter, as described in the Vaishnava Agamas, all these are combined into one whole in the modern concept of Vishnu and the first and second of them probably come down from the lithic ages.

Kāli, the world-mother, is the result of the synthesis of the various local goddesses into the idea of the Divine Power (Śakti), which causes the evolution of matter, the power which shapes matter into the ordered universe of beings and which keeps them going till the great Pralaya dissolves Name and Form.

The ancient, as well as modern worship of Siva and Vishṇu and Ambā, are forms of fireless worship and are described in the three sets of books called the Agamas. They are utterly different from and opposed to the Vedic fire-cult. The Vedic gods formed a democracy ; Indra and Varuṇa, Vāyu and Sūrya, Mitra and Savitā, were all of equal status. The god of each Agama is the supreme Person, demanding the whole-hearted devotion (*ekabhakti*) of the worshipper. The worship according to the Agama and that according to the Veda (and its culmination, the Vedānta) were rival, inimical cults ; the former absolutely "fireless", and the latter, literally or symbolically, a fire-cult. The Vedic cult regarded the division of the Aryas into four varṇas as absolutely indispensable, the Agama-rites in old days ignored this social organization. The worship of Siva or Vishṇu or Śakti in temples or houses was considered a heresy by the Vedantis, till in the tenth century Yāmunāchārya wrote the *Āgama prāmāṇya* and Rāmānujachārya in the next century blended the Vaishnava rites and concepts and the Vedic practices and Vedanta tenets into one whole. Thus started Neo-Hinduism, which is a development from the fireless cults of the Neolithic Ages, with the social organization of the fire-cult of the Iron Age and the merest traces of the elaborate fire-worship of the rishis, imposed on them.

The gorgeous ritual of the fire-rite arose and spread in Aryāvartta, north of the Vindhyas, probably five or six milleniums ago, and began to decline with the destruction of the Kshatriya dynasties in the cataclysm of the Mahabhārata War in the second millenium B.C. The fire-rite was confined, when it lasted, to a section of the people, called the Āryas, the bulk of the people being the Dasyus, who adhered to their fireless rites. When the concept of fire being the mouth of the gods was developed, when sacrifices to them were first offered through fire, it is impossible to determine. Purūravas, the first king who may be regarded as a historical personage and who was separated from the Nandas by about one hundred generations and who hence lived before 3000 B.C., is said in the Vedas and the Puranas, to have been the first king who started with the help of rishis the worship with the "three fires", i.e., to have begun the elaborate fire-rituals, since called the Śrauta. European scholars believe that the fire-rite was evolved outside India and was brought into the country by invaders belonging to a foreign race, to which they have applied the Indian cult-name, the Arya. Now there is absolutely no evidence, historical or literary or anthropological, to justify this theory. Anthropology knows of no Aryan race. The existence of a highly developed civilization in Sind and Punjab, as is proved by the recent explorations at Harappa and Maheñjo Daro, the five or six milleniums ago, is fatal to the theory of an invasion or conquest of ancient India by foreign intruders in those ancient times. There is no trace in the Vedic hymns of recollections of a foreign habitat of the ancient Aryas. On the contrary the Vedic sacrifices which belonged to the Iron Age contain evidences of growth from neolithic times in India. The resemblance of the buffalo-sacrifices of the Savaras to sacrifices referred to in the Vedic hymns has been pointed out earlier. Other traces of neolithic customs can be easily found. The site of the yajña is consecrated by dragging a frog on stone till it is killed. The animal sacrificed is tied to a wooden post (*yūpa*) and even to-day not killed with iron weapons; its 'nine holes' are stopped and then it is clubbed to death. The sacredness of this method of killing the sacrificial victim proves that it originated before iron was used as the material for tools. That earthenware pots and wooden utensils alone are sacred enough to be used in the hall of sacrifice is another proof that the fire-sacrifices had their roots in neolithic practices. Many another custom of the Lithic Age can be traced in the Vedic rites.

CONCLUSION

The chronological limits of the Neolithic Age are entirely a matter of guess. The glacial deposits that help to fix the age of neolithic sites in Europe are wanting in India. Considering the extreme slowness of human advancement in lithic times, 20000 B.C. to 5000 B.C., cannot be a very wrong estimate of the date of New Stone Age. Iron was discovered before the rise of the Arya cult, which was, in my opinion, not later than five thousand or six thousand years ago.

The Stone Age is still very much with us. In our villages, shooting stones from slings is still widely used, both as a volley to disperse a crowd and as an artillery preparation for burglary. Singlestick (with wands of the male bamboo) is still played and experts in singlestick use it as a means of offence and defence; schools of the noble art of fencing with the bamboo stick still exist in various places where secret methods of advancing on the foe, jealously guarded by professors of fencing from becoming known to all and sundry, are taught to favourite pupils; by these methods one man can disarm and lay low a hundred opponents. The bow, made by bending the split bamboo, is still found in several village homes; clay balls, dried in the sun, are shot from these bows for driving off, from fruit trees, monkeys and other depredators. The holy thread of the Brāhmanas is even to-day spun with spindles made of the spine of the coconut leaf and weighted with a stone disc; the use of an iron tool at any stage of its manufacture will make the thread lose its holiness. Most of the appliances used by the housewife are of stone or wood, for things made of these materials are unpollutable, or if polluted, can be restored to sanctity by merely washing with water, whereas metal goods polluted by touch have to be burnt in fire, before being used again. The principal idol in temples is the one made of stone or wood; images of metal are for the relatively more secular purpose of being paraded in the streets. The chief objects of domestic worship are the quartz lingam and the fossile ammonite (a bone turned into stone). Numerous other customs coming down from the Lithic Ages may be discovered by the curious enquirer, old customs being distinguished from later ones by their sacrosanct character.

LIST OF PLATES.

PLATE I.

PALÆOLITHIC TOOLS.

2204-7	...	Large axe—guillotine type.
2204-8	...	Axe—Madras type.
3248	...	Do.
2204-5	...	Spear-head type.
2204-9	...	Narrow pointed oval type—sharp edges all round.
2204-22	...	Pointed sharp-sided pebble-butt type.
2204-10	.	Broad pointed oval type.
205	...	Oval type, edges rather sharp all round.
2204-21	...	Do. very sharp edges all round.

PLATE II.

PALÆOLITHIC TOOLS.

1051	...	Chisel.
402	...	Do. square body, round angles, perfect edge.
1993	...	Do. cross cut edge, thick body.
409	...	Do. with thick butt.
412	...	Do.
1047	...	Do.
1045	...	Do.
403	...	Do. narrow-edged, thick body.
689	...	Do. thick body.

NEOLITHIC TOOLS.

2149	...	Chisel, small, shapely, square sides.
1044	...	Do. elliptical edge.
2662	...	Scraper, thin long type.
987	...	Pick or hoe.
1122-A	...	Whetstone for celts.
2655	..	Adze.
2373	...	Chisel flake.
2374	...	Javelin head.
429	...	Scraper.

PLATE III.

NEOLITHIC FINDS.

1212	...	Corn-crusher.
1548	...	Lingam—flat cone grooved vertically.
1549	...	Do. cone on cylinder.
3237	...	Disc.
2606-1	...	Flake-knife.
886	...	Scraper.
80	...	Saw.

PLATE IV

ELEPHANT-SHAPED FUNERAL VASE.

N.B.—These plates have been taken from *Indian Pre-historic and Protohistoric Antiquities* by Robert Bruce Foote.

Plate I.

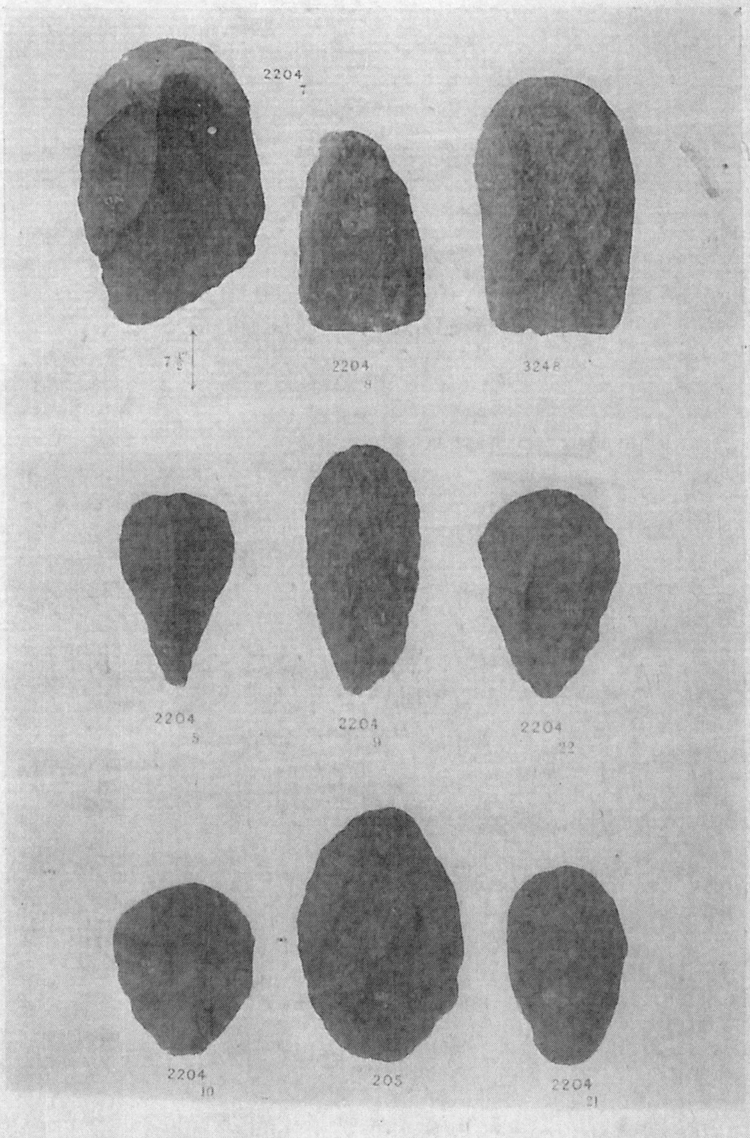

PLATE II.

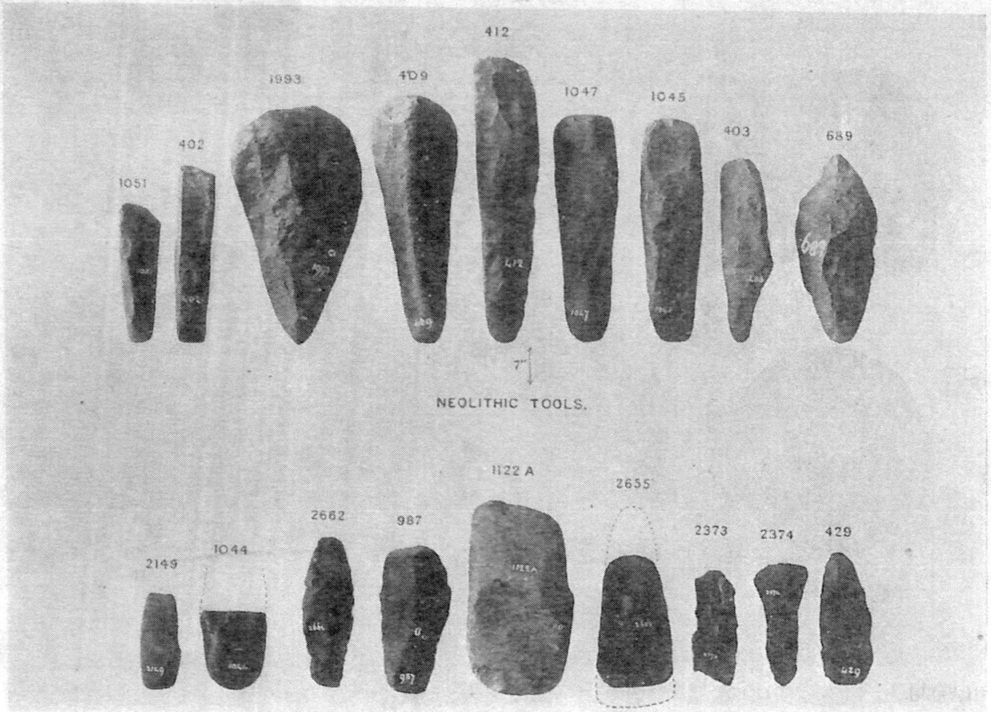

NEOLITHIC TOOLS.

PLATE III.

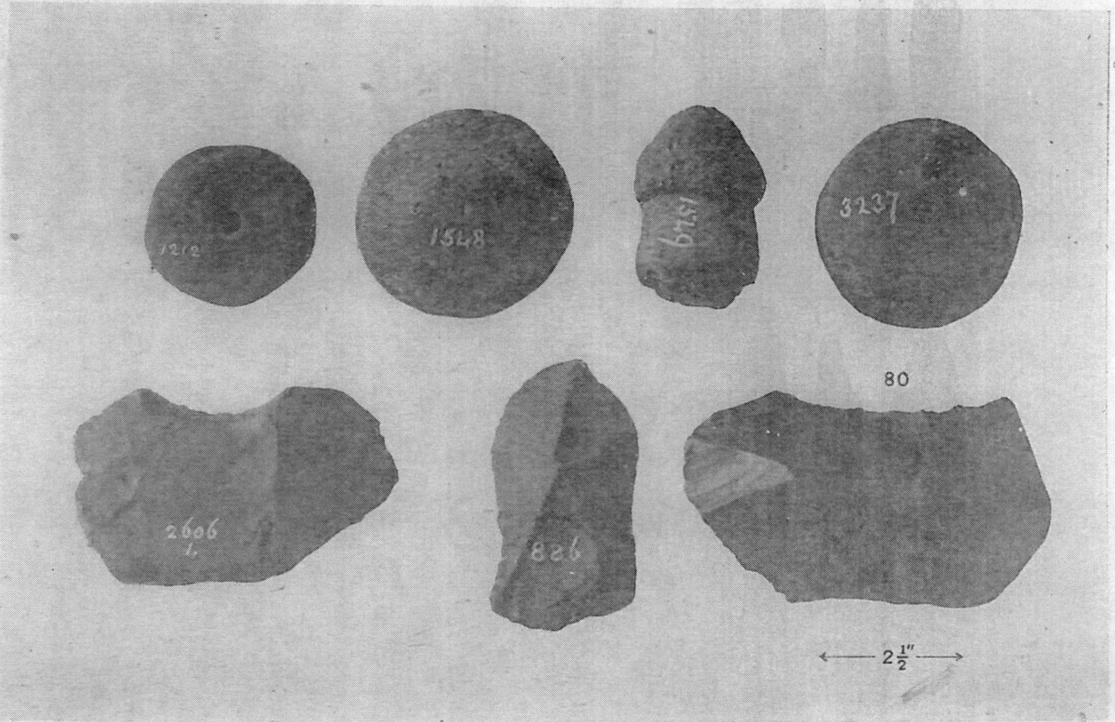

Plate IV.

MAP OF INDIA : PALÆOLITHIC SITES

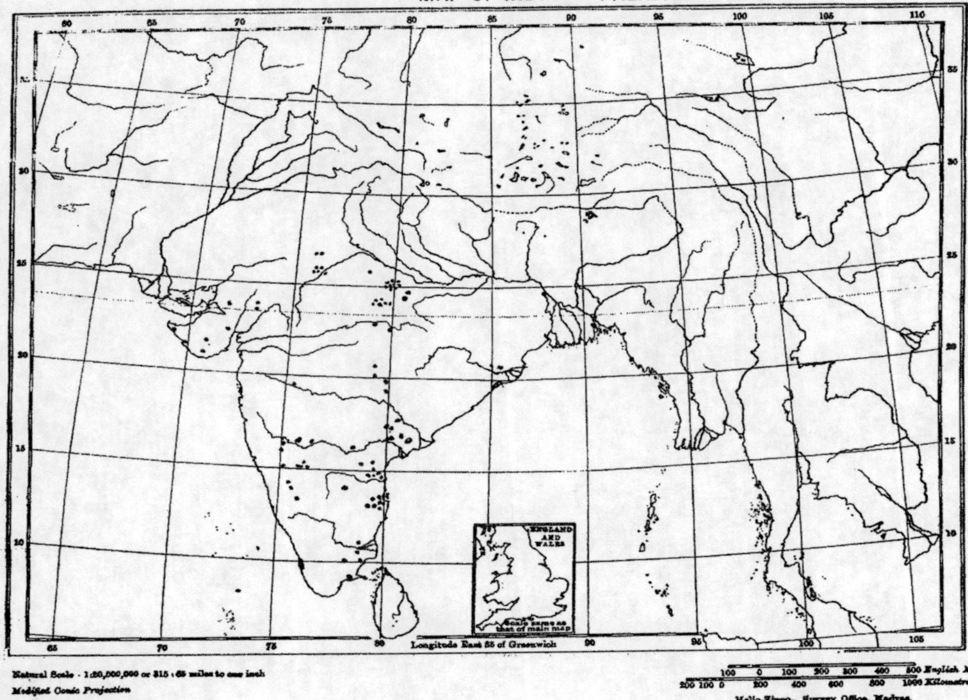

Natural Scale - 1:20,000,000 or 315 : 65 miles to one inch

Modified Conic Projection

Reg. No. 716/2 Copies 500

Hello-Zinco., Survey Office, Madras.
1927